"Hoorah. One of the nation's leading writers for and about children explains everything you need to know for an outstanding kindergarten."
 —Chester E. Finn, Jr.
  Assistant Secretary for Research and Improvement
  U.S. Department of Education

"Jean Marzollo has written a practical book that will be useful to both teachers and parents. In nontechnical language she has provided a philosophy of kindergarten education, describing the kindergarten as a place where significant learning can take place without undue pressure for academic achievement."
 —Bernard Spodek
  Professor of Early Childhood Education, University of Illinois

"Easy reading and down to earth, this book avails its readers of the most current, theoretically sound methods of instruction for kindergarten to date."
 —Debarrí Borrego
  Full-day Kindergarten Teacher, Cordova, New Mexico

"In *The New Kindergarten* readers find ideas quickly and follow clear, well illustrated instructions for easy implementation. The new teacher will gain helpful information in classroom set-up, curriculum and planning, while the experienced teacher will get a much needed burst of new energy to add to an existing program."
 —Ellen Booth Church
  Early Childhood Education, State University of New York

"Marzollo shows how content of high academic value is achieved through active, playfilled, integrated activities while she deftly combats the pressures to push down sterile, inappropriate activities from the elementary grades to the 'garden of children.' " —Elizabeth Sulzby
  Associate Professor of Education, University of Michigan

"This book helps to clarify the delicate relationship between meaningful activity and educational goals for children. The illustrations by Irene Trivas capture the wonderful nature of children."
 —Olivia Rivera
  Early Childhood Coordinator, Albuquerque Public Schools

What people are saying about
THE NEW KINDERGARTEN

**Other books written by Jean Marzollo
and illustrated by Irene Trivas**

Birthday Parties for Children

Superkids

Supertot

Learning Through Play (Coauthored with Janice Lloyd)

THE NEW KINDERGARTEN
Full-Day, Child-Centered, Academic

A Book for Teachers, Administrators,
Practice Teachers, Teacher Aides, and Parents

JEAN MARZOLLO
Illustrated by IRENE TRIVAS

HARPER & ROW, Publishers, New York
Cambridge, Philadelphia, San Francisco, Washington
London, Mexico City, São Paulo, Singapore, Sydney

Portions of this book have appeared in altered form in *Parents*.

FIRST EDITION

Designer: Lydia Link

Copyeditor: Libby Kessman

Library of Congress Cataloging-in-Publication Data

Marzollo, Jean. 1942–
  The new kindergarten.

  1. Full-day kindergarten—United States.
2. Kindergarten—Curricula. I. Title.
LB1180.M37 1987   372'.218   87-45071
ISBN 0-06-015786-0

87 88 89 90 91 MPC 10 9 8 7 6 5 4 3 2 1

For

Ellen Booth Church

J. M.

———

For

Karina

I. T.

Contents

Acknowledgments

With special thanks to: Ellen Booth Church, Dr. Joanne Marien, Betsy Rasa, Fran Dawson, Carol Kiefer, Dr. Dudley Hare, Jr., Dr. Bernard Spodek, Joanne Oppenheim, Kate McMullan, Della Rowland, Dr. Leslie Williams, Dr. Olivia Saracho, Dr. Elizabeth Sulzby, Dr. Joe Frost, Beth Kolehmainen, Elizabeth Crow, Debarrí Borrego, Rose Cordova, Barbara Welther, Margaret Griffeth, Donald Rotkin, Dorothy Silver, Lorraine Volpe, Ursula Davis, Carol Carson, and John Lent.

Introduction

Kindergarten is changing. No longer a half-day "practice" session designed to help five-year-olds make the transition from home to school, in many districts kindergarten today resembles other elementary grades. It is a full-day program (usually from about 8:30 to 3:00) with its own special goals and curriculum.

The kindergarten curriculum is more academic than it used to be, not falsely so—with a flashy but superficial program of letters and numbers—but rather a genuinely academic curriculum in which children are taught to think, solve problems, share ideas, and write and read *on their own level*.

The new kindergarten retains the best of the old-fashioned kindergarten—an atmosphere of play and nurturing care in which children are treated as children. In today's classroom, however, play may be more oriented toward learning. Teachers promote "work/play"—the kind of serious play that children do when they are painting, building with blocks, modeling clay dinosaurs, counting beads, and writing stories.

Taken alone, none of these ideas is new: neither full-day kindergarten nor child-centered kindergarten nor academic kindergarten. What *is* new is that all three are being combined successfully today.

Various factors have brought about the change. First, in recent years many parents have felt that their five-year-olds, who already have spent a year or more in day care or nursery school, are ready for something more challenging. Such parents want more academic experiences for their children.

Second, many working parents, whose preschoolers are accustomed to day care, have found the half-day of kindergarten offered by public schools something of a step backward. They want a longer school day.

Third, in recent years many kindergarten teachers have found that their five-year-olds are ready for a fuller, richer school program. Not a first-grade program, they are quick to point out; good teachers know that fives are still fives. Kindergartners need a special program of their own, one that's intellectually and emotionally suited to their wonderful five-year-old abilities. Research in recent years has supported what good teachers already know: *that children learn best when they can direct their own learning.*

Armed with new ideas and techniques, teachers have realized that with more time they can teach today's five-year-olds better and more. As one teacher put it, "In a typical half-day session, children take off their coats, play a little, do an activity, go to the bathroom, have a snack, go outside, come inside, settle down, listen to a story, clean up, get their coats on, and go home. There isn't time for meaningful hands-on science experiments. There isn't time to develop language and writing projects based on actual classroom experiences."

Fourth, many states and local school districts have been persuaded that children graduating from full-day kindergarten become better learners in elementary school, especially first grade. The costs of running a full-day kindergarten program can be offset by the gains of teaching children earlier and by spotting children who need special help earlier—the basic theory being that the sooner teachers catch problems, the easier it is to address them.

Thus persuaded, officials around the country have established public school full-day kindergartens. (They have also established variations of the full-day: extended day, full-day every other day, and so on.) The results are mixed. In districts where the necessary groundwork is done wisely, programs fare well. In districts where kindergarten programs are tossed down from above with little thought and inadequate attention to research, programs fare poorly.

Where change has been mishandled, you see that children have been switched from old-fashioned work/play areas to desks in rows. At their desks they work, without a sense of play, in workbooks: first in a reading workbook, then in a math workbook, then in a science workbook, then in a social studies workbook. The children may look academically engaged but in fact they don't learn very much that's meaningful or lasting. Moreover, while at their desks, they are denied precious time to learn the way they learn best: *actively, concretely, and autonomously*.

The new truly academic kindergarten is child-centered, not teacher-centered. How a child-centered kindergarten works is the subject of this book. In my work as editor of Scholastic's *Let's Find Out* kindergarten magazine for fifteen years, I have witnessed the development of many new full-day, child-centered, academic kindergartens across the country. The teachers of these programs are more thrilled than ever about their work.

Unfortunately, I also hear from teachers who are more unhappy than ever—teachers who don't know how to teach a full-day kindergarten and teachers who are required to teach in ways they feel are wrong.

It's a crisis time for kindergarten. Teachers and administrators whose programs are weak need to spend time observing in classrooms where programs are strong. Teachers and administrators whose programs are strong need to share them. All districts need to ask themselves if their programs improve the lives of young children.

Hopefully, this book, *The New Kindergarten*, will help teachers, administrators, aides, practice teachers, and parents understand what a full-day, child-centered, and academic kindergarten can be like. With shared knowledge and goals, such people can cooperate to create and implement full-day kindergartens in which children blossom intellectually, socially, creatively, and physically.

Chapter One

The Purpose of Kindergarten Today

The purpose of the new kindergarten is to teach children a rich, meaningful, and balanced curriculum of skills and information through age-appropriate activities that encourage the children to want to learn more. Several points can be made about this goal:

1. "A rich, meaningful, and balanced curriculum of skills and information" encompasses intellectual, social, creative, and physical learning. "Rich" means that the curriculum is full of worthy content, "meaningful" means that the content has meaning for children, and "balanced" means that the curriculum covers language arts (oral language, listening, writing, and reading), social studies, science, math, art, music, and physical education.

2. "Age-appropriate activities" means that activities in the new kindergarten suit four-, five-, and six-year-olds, who learn best through concrete activities that they can direct. What guides a good kindergarten teacher's selection of activities for her children is the question: *Is the activity too old for the children, too young for them, or just right for their developmental needs?* ("Developmental needs" means the needs of a child at a given stage of development.) If the children would like to do the activity again, chances are the activity is age-appropriate.

3. Though it should apply to other grades as well, the phrase "in such a way that they want to learn more" is especially crucial for kindergarten and prekindergarten children. Young children are naturally curious. If their curiosity is turned off in the early years by inappropriate instruction, they may establish negative attitudes about themselves as learners. Good kindergarten teachers do not stifle their children's natural curiosity; they build upon it so that their children *continue* as enthusiastic learners.

Full-day kindergarten programs that fail, do so for various reasons; it is not always the teacher's fault. In some cases, teachers who are used to the routine of teaching two half-day kindergarten classes a day suddenly find themselves told to teach one class for a full day. The longer day reveals an enormous lack of substance in the basic kindergarten curriculum. It had been one thing to have a state guide that mandated science topics, such as weather, rocks, dinosaurs, and the five senses, but with sufficient time now to teach the topics, experienced teachers discover that they don't know how to do it. Many teachers trained in early childhood education are able to figure out answers on their own, but others, especially upper-grade teachers suddenly transferred to kindergarten, are understandably confused.

"Where are the textbooks?" they ask, finding it hard to believe that on the kindergarten level there are few—for good reason. Kindergartners, in general, don't read, and they can't write answers to questions at the end of chapters. Kindergarten teachers have to teach through activities, not textbooks. "But what activities?" asks a transferred sixth-grade teacher.

In schools where the elementary school principal understands kindergarten, the principal can supply some answers, but principals who lack early childhood training are unsure. Before full-day kindergarten, they didn't need to know that much about kindergarten; now they do.

In some states, legislators, inspired by the educational excellence movement, have passed laws mandating goals for the kindergarten curriculum. The mandates are a mixed blessing. In some cases, they lend structure and

credence to the kindergarten program. Yet, unfortunately, because many of the legislators themselves don't know that much about kindergarten, many of the mandates passed are falsely academic and not readily teachable in a child-centered classroom.

Unrealistic mandates can force a teacher to compartmentalize her time rigidly in order to cover all the mandates. In other cases, mandates may force a teacher to teach material she doesn't think is appropriate for her children's ability level. Good teachers are frustrated when they feel forced to give first priority to subjects and second priority to children's developmental needs. When mandates are found to be impractical in the classroom, legislators must be free to change and improve them.

Misguided mandated kindergarten curricula that are doing damage now will do even more damage in the future as increasing numbers of children enter school, causing a national teacher shortage. The possibilities of new, inexperienced teachers following mandates without knowing which ones are better than others is disturbing. What's also disturbing is that publishers, rushing to serve the expanding kindergarten market, are designing materials with state mandates in mind. For the sake of the children, it is crucial that teachers and administrators familiar with the real needs of five-year-olds decide which materials are appropriate for the classroom.

Starting a Successful Full-Day, Child-Centered, Academic Kindergarten Program

Because full-day kindergarten is a relatively new phenomenon compared to, say, full-day first grade, and because no one class or school is exactly like another, teachers, parents, and administrators usually have to create new full-day kindergarten programs themselves. Though the process of creating a new program from scratch can be frustrating, it has many benefits. By not adopting a program handed down from "on high," teachers create a program they believe in. It's theirs. They thought it through, and they take responsibility for it. The teachers want their program to work so they are apt to improve it willingly as they go along.

Teachers who believe in their programs train new staff members enthusiastically and get the most out of workshops, conventions, and in-service training. They also can help to train other teachers in other districts, thus gaining prestige for their own district and feeling a personal sense of pride and accomplishment. In good schools there is a sense of excitement as teachers share new ideas for activities and use of materials.

The worst way to plan a full-day kindergarten program is to take a first-grade curriculum and move it downstairs. Children are pressured to learn material that's too hard for them, and at the same time they are denied the rich assortment of concrete activities they should be experiencing in kindergarten. Young children learn best when they can figure out problems firsthand. They suffer educationally when such experiences are taken away in favor of paper, pencil, and the three R's.

What is said about the little girl with the curl in her forehead can be said about full-day kindergarten: when it's good, it is very, very good, but when it is bad, it is horrid.

What Parents Can Do to Help: Understand and Participate

Parents who are not used to full-day kindergarten have different reactions to the idea of one in their district. Some feel their children aren't old enough to be gone from home seven and a half hours a day, including transportation. They lament the loss of intimate parenting time. Others feel their children will benefit with increased intellectual stimulation, and many working parents breathe a sigh of relief upon hearing that their children will be supervised productively for a longer period of time at no cost other than the taxes they were already paying.

Districts starting full-day kindergartens often find it helpful to involve parents on committees right from the start so that parents feel a part of the start-up process. Parent discussion groups can help reluctant parents to feel better and all parents to understand the purpose of kindergarten. Some parents are expecting the three R's. They have a hard time comprehending how playing with blocks, making constructions with junk materials, and cooking in the classroom is educational. To them, this is just more "play." Such suspicions may be alleviated by arranging a visit to a neighboring good full-day kindergarten classroom so parents can see five-year-olds in action and observe how teachers work with them. After a full-day program is started, parents should be encouraged to visit the school to see how their children are doing.

Good teachers encourage parent visits because they find that the more parents see what's going on, the more they understand the purpose of kindergarten. The more they understand, the more they can be involved. Parents can help a teacher by sending in requested materials, chaperoning on trips, and volunteering to help with special projects, such as baking and sharing special hobbies.

What Kindergarten Teachers Want Parents to Understand

Kindergarten teachers want parents to understand that they are concerned with children's intellectual learning and also with their social, creative, and physical growth. They know that the needs of the "whole" child are important.

Kindergarten teachers want parents to understand that play is instructional. Play-as-a-method-of-instruction ("work/play") is not exactly the same thing as free play. Free play is a time when children can choose whatever they want to do.

Play-as-a-method-of-instruction or "work/play" refers to the type of activity through which children construct their own learning. For example, the fact that two halves make a whole is an abstraction for young children, and because it is an abstraction they are not interested. But to discover the same fact by playing with blocks or measuring cups is a different matter entirely. That's interesting! A skillful teacher asks children to bring her examples of how two halves make a whole. To do the activity, children have to think for themselves. In this way, good teachers ask children to think for themselves. They don't tell the answers; they let children discover them, which is more fun for the children—and more effective.

Both types of play are important for children to experience because play is concrete, firsthand, and active. Five-year-olds need to use their senses to learn. They are not at the stage where they can just hear about something or see a picture of it and know what it's about.

Good kindergarten teachers provide play materials and activities that are "developmentally appropriate," meaning that they fit a child's developmental stage.

Work, Play, and Tests

"Believing that kindergartners should major in more than sandbox, the school superintendent in Minneapolis ordered a competency test for youngsters before they could be promoted to first grade," reads an article in *The New York Times,* January 5, 1986. "The oral test, said to be the first of its kind for kindergartners in the country, measured such areas as recognition of the alphabet, colors, the counting of numbers up to 31, and the addition of coins to total 10 cents. About 15 percent of the 3,000 pupils—460—flunked in May 1984 and were candidates to be left back. Opportunities to make up work were offered, including summer school. The final say on whether pupils were ready for the first grade was given to their teachers."

The reason this item was news was that the test was the first of its kind. What we, as parents and teachers, may find worth pondering is this: Five, ten, or twenty years from now, will such a test be common? If such a radical change occurs in schooling, it should be one that parents and teachers have questioned.

We need to ask questions, such as: Can a standardized test reliably assess what children have learned in kindergarten? Many educators say no. If tests are given to kindergartners, will schools begin to teach "to the test" so that their children pass? In so doing, will schools have to shrink or eliminate parts of their program in order to make time for teaching "to the test"? What parts of the program will be shrunk or eliminated—playing at the sand table? What if experts say that playing at the sandbox is educational in demonstrable ways that are hard to assess with standardized tests?

More questions: What is the obligation of schools to make sure that kindergartners graduate with the skills they will need to succeed in first

grade? Do some children need a considerable measure of structure, drill, and discipline in kindergarten in order to learn? Would other children find such discipline deadening and superfluous?

As we, parents and teachers, try to answer these complex questions, we may find our viewpoints polarizing and ourselves rigidly taking sides. One side may accuse the other side of wanting nothing but "play." The other side accuses the first side of wanting nothing but "work." This is silly. We have created a false dichotomy between socialization and learning. All we have to do is watch and talk with children in order to see that they differ widely and that we have to meet *their* needs, not our needs for ideological absolutes.

Some children need a more structured classroom in which they can take things one at a time. Others need more freedom to explore. All children benefit from a combination of work and play. Kids need structure *and* freedom, and that is the rub. Achieving the proper balance for each child is the teacher's art. The best thing about the Minneapolis test may be that the final judgment is left up to the teacher.

Kindergarten means "child's garden." As stated at the beginning of the chapter, the purpose of the new kindergarten is to teach children a rich, meaningful, and balanced curriculum of skills and information through age-appropriate activities that encourage children to want to learn more. This is the child's garden where today's child wants and needs to be.

Chapter Two

The Content of the Kindergarten Curriculum: Subject Areas, Skills, and Themes

The kindergarten curriculum includes seven main subject areas: language arts (oral language, listening, writing, and reading), social studies, science, math, art, music, and physical education.

These subject areas can be integrated through unifying themes that children enjoy exploring. Such themes may, but do not have to, coordinate with the time of year. Ten themes are presented in this book as examples of how the thematic approach to curriculum can be used in the classroom. The themes presented are suggested for certain months, but teachers should feel free to schedule them at other times. These are by no means the only themes appropriate for kindergarten. There are many other themes, and some of the best ones are those conceived by enthusiastic teachers—creative themes such as bears, fasteners, spaces and places, light.

Skills taught in kindergarten overlap subject areas. Counting, for example, may be practiced during a discussion of "The Three Bears" and experimenting with plants may follow a reading of "Jack and the Beanstalk." Kindergarten skills are not just taught once and dropped, but rather they are taught and reviewed over and over as they naturally occur in activities and discussions. Because they are presented in context, they are meaningful to the children.

AND THEN THE LITTLE BEAR...

In the new kindergarten children explore new topics in an organized fashion. A general method of activity children explore is to explore materials, record the results, and discuss the recordings with each other. In the process children use many skills, such as discriminating shapes and sounds, sorting, classifying, counting, sequencing, seriation, comparing, identifying, recording, and self-expression. (For a list of skills appropriate for kindergarten, see Appendix.)

Subject areas, skills, and themes are integrated by the teacher in the new kindergarten. Blending them together takes creativity, knowledge of content, and, most of all, sensitivity to children's needs. It isn't easy. But good kindergarten teachers can do the trick.

In this book ideas used in the new kindergarten are presented with pictures and simple instructions. Teachers should feel free to adapt and expand upon the ideas to suit their children and locale.

Language Arts

Language arts encompasses oral language, listening, reading, and writing. In the new kindergarten these four essential aspects of communication are integrated, not only with each other but with the rest of the curriculum. Successful activities in the classroom foster oral language experience as children share their ideas and discoveries with each other. Oral language experiences in turn foster listening skills as children learn to listen to each other. Having ideas one wants to share leads naturally to a desire to record ideas in some fashion. In the new kindergarten teachers encourage children to record their ideas in a variety of ways: with blocks, with clay, with paint and other art

materials, with graphs, with rebus messages, and with writing done at whatever level children are at. Some draw, some scribble, some string letters together any which way, some invent ways to spell that make sense (sm for swim), and some rare few *can* spell. It doesn't matter as long as a child *wants* to write. Often, a five-year-old will use several methods and be able to "read" them all afterward.

Reading

Children come to kindergarten with a great range of abilities. A rare child or two in a class is already reading, having begun the process with questions about print in books parents have read aloud. As these questions were answered, the child learned to read. Such early readers are called "spontaneous readers," and they are a source of amazement and pride to teachers and parents alike.

A few children don't catch on to the reading game until they're seven or eight. These children are perfectly normal, just a little late. The old adage "You can take a horse to water, but you can't make him drink" applies well to these children. If you are a parent or teacher of one of these children, don't nag. Instead, soothe yourself and the child by remembering that children learn to walk and talk at different times, and that late bloomers catch up.

Some kindergarten children have learning disabilities, specific and identifiable neurological and/or emotional problems that interfere with reading progress. Many problems, such as the inability to concentrate and write letters correctly, are natural to young children and will be outgrown in time. Certain problems, however, need special attention. We are fortunate to live

at a time when special education teachers can help children with learning problems. Federal law 94-142 guarantees special education programs for children who require them.

Most children learn to read words and sentences when they are six—that is, in first grade. This is as it always has been. Developmentally, children haven't changed. In the new kindergarten, however, teachers realize that most younger children are interested in reading and eager to "read" on their own level. This may mean that, while they do not understand letter/sound association (phonics), they are able to read individual letters, read their own drawings and scribbles as stories, read rebus symbols, and read memorized words and stories. Good teachers find out what their children are "reading" and help them make the most of their accomplishments.

To help children move on, teachers give them interesting materials that fit their abilities. Interesting materials include well-written and well-illustrated picture books read and discussed at a daily storytime, picture cards with simple labels, poster-size books with big print that the teacher can point to as she reads aloud, and rebus puzzles in which certain words are represented by pictures that the children can "read."

Becoming a Nation of Readers, a remarkably well-written and understandable government report published in 1985 (you can order it from the National Institute of Education, Washington, DC 20208) summarizes research on reading and has this to say about reading in kindergarten: "What the child who is least ready for systematic reading instruction needs most is ample experience with oral and printed language, and early opportunities to write." Oral language means talking, and printed language means looking at books—both activities that parents can and should do with their children at home.

Writing

Whereas children used to be discouraged from learning to write until first grade, when presumably they would be better able to spell and form letters, in the new kindergarten they are being encouraged to write in whatever way they can manage, and spell however they are inclined. "Invented spelling," such as "Ga" for "Grandma," is the result, much the way invented words ("ba" for "bottle") are spoken by babies.

The point, say teachers, is that the children want to write, so why hold them back? If we tell kids their letters are sloppy and their spelling is wrong, they won't keep trying. If we encourage them with praise, they will.

"Cow," said my nephew Ricky at the age of two, trying to pronounce my husband Claudio's name. "Cow!" we all said. Not a relative among us would have thought to criticize Ricky and demand that he repeat the name until he could say it correctly.

"I Wnt Pl" writes a child under a drawing of a big blue blob. Later, she proudly "reads" her paper to her classmates. "I went swimming in a pool," she says with her eyes on her letters. Every child in the class listens attentively, and when the sharing of the papers is over, no one other than the teacher seems to have noticed how many different levels of writing ability were demonstrated.

Are these children reading and writing? Well, no, not exactly. But they are definitely learning to read and write, just as Ricky was learning to speak when he said "Cow" for "Claudio." Are the kids enjoying themselves? Do they want to do more? Yes, if you accept their efforts with joy.

Opportunities to write in kindergarten may entail dictating stories in a group to teachers who write them in big letters on big pads of "language experience" paper. Sometimes the sentences are dictated one per child, each written in a different color. The children remember their colors and their lines, and, lo and behold, they are able later on to read their lines aloud.

Kindergarten teachers allow for a great deal of flexibility in writing and reading activities, always keeping in mind that some children are advanced, some are beginning, and most are in between.

Formal, or systematic, reading instruction on letters and letter sounds is appropriate in kindergarten, provided that the materials are developmentally appropriate and that they supplement active experiences. As one kindergarten teacher told me, "My district requires that I use a reading workbook with the children. So I use it this way: I give my children many concrete activities before they ever see the reading workbook page. When they finally get to the page, the children know how to do it, and they all succeed."

Math

Kindergarten teachers teach math in concrete ways, using materials that give children firsthand experience with counting and thinking. Children learn math in formal and informal lessons all day long. Formal learning may follow a plan established by the school curriculum. Informal learning occurs spontaneously as children compare how old they are, count how many baby gerbils were born, and learn to solve problems by thinking logically.

In formal lessons the children may work at their desks or tables with counting chips or abacuses (a Chinese counting frame). They may measure the growth of plants with popsicle sticks and record the results on workbook sheets.

Sometimes the children may work in math centers, where they can

experience abstract concepts such as addition, subtraction, and fractions by playing with dominoes, Cuisenaire rods, sequence blocks, number puzzles, measuring cups, and toy clocks.

Centers are special areas for independent learning around the room. In some classrooms teachers rotate children in and out of the centers at various times of the day and in various ways. Most classrooms have a math center, a science center, a language arts/reading center, a library center, a housekeeping or dramatic play center, a block center, an art center, and a game center. In addition, some have computer centers (there are at least a dozen good, interesting computer software programs for the kindergarten level—see Appendix), a listening center (where children listen through headsets to records and tapes—often in conjunction with books), and a music center.

A child working (or playing—an actively engaged child doesn't make the distinction the way adults do) at a math center may be exploring materials freely or carrying out a task directed by the teacher and further explained by a *task card,* which is more or less a picture recipe that reminds the child of the problem to solve. The task may be to sort a mixture of seeds into categories and then to count them.

The end result of a math activity is often recorded so that it can be shared later with others. Kindergarten teachers show children many ways to record an experience: by drawing pictures, by measuring with yarn or Legos, by taking Polaroid photographs of the steps in a process and pasting them in order on paper, by dictating one's thoughts to someone who can write them down, and by a special math activity called graphing.

Graphing is an effective math activity that can be done on many levels. At the beginning of the year, the teacher might say, "Let's find out how we came to school today." She puts a toy car on the floor and asks all those who

came by car to stand behind it. Then she puts a toy bus on the floor and asks all those who came by bus to stand behind it. Last she puts a toy figure of a person on the floor and asks all those who walked to stand behind it.

In their three lines, the children look around curiously at each other, and the teacher poses a question. "Which line has the most children?" The concept of "most" is difficult on the abstract level, but easy to discuss when you're talking about real bodies. At some point, the teacher might give each child a counting chip and ask them to place the chips, one at a time, on a graph with three columns atop pictures of a car, a bus, and a walker. The children can see that the chips represent themselves; they can "read" the graphs, which have helped them make the difficult transfer from the concrete to the abstract. The more children graph, the better they get at it; and they like the work/play of graphing, especially when they can start with something concrete first, such as shoes, leaves, toys, books, dinosaur models, and monster pictures.

The most important aspect of math is logical thinking. Good kindergarten teachers frequently ask children questions that make them think. They don't tell children the answers; they wait for the children to reach them on their own. The questions they ask are likely to be ones that cannot be answered with "yes," or "no," or a one-word answer. Such thought-provoking questions often begin with phrases, such as: "What would happen if . . ." and "How can we do . . ."

Science

Science on the kindergarten level offers five-year-olds a chance to shine. Their special ways of thinking are wonderfully flexible and creative, and they can

think up many experiments that are interesting to execute. Born experimenters, children like to try things out for themselves *by* themselves because they instinctively know that this is how they learn best. The noted Swiss educational psychologist Jean Piaget knew this too and stressed throughout his work the importance of autonomy in a child's learning. As they work with children, teachers (and parents too) can encourage and preserve the experimental thought processes of children by giving them the freedom to work problems through on their own.

In kindergarten children should have experiences hypothesizing and predicting, manipulating objects, posing questions, researching answers, imagining, investigating, and inventing. A good kindergarten teacher encourages the scientific process. Children, for example, experiment with things that sink and float. Each child can be asked to find in the classroom two objects: one that the child thinks will float and one that the child thinks will sink. The child draws his predictions on a worksheet, executes the experiment, and records the results. The process is intriguing, inexpensive, and scientifically instructive as to facts and procedures. It's also fun.

When teaching science, kindergarten teachers once again ask children thought-provoking questions, not just "Did you ever see the snow before?" (which can be answered with a simple yes or no) but also "Where do you think snow comes from?" During the ensuing discussion, teachers encourage not just one right answer (convergent thinking), but many answers (divergent thinking). They encourage children to brainstorm, listing all the ideas they can think of. Five-year-olds excel at this.

Kindergarten teachers aid and abet children's natural creativity. Instead of looking for the one "right" answer, they welcome all answers, such as: "The snow is pieces of clouds" and "The snow comes from snowmen in the

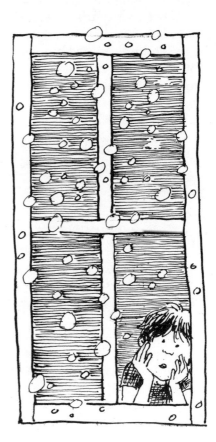

sky." After a stimulating discussion, good teachers ask children to record (draw, scribble, write with invented spelling) their ideas on paper.

Kindergarten teachers know that teaching is asking, not telling. They encourage children to find out correct answers for themselves. "How can we find out what snow is made of?" they ask the children. And as experiments are being carried out, the teachers stay flexible because they have learned through experience to expect the unexpected. If there's a surprise fire drill during a lesson on snow and ice, kindergarten teachers know that when the children return to the classroom, they are going to want to talk about the fire drill.

Social Studies

Social studies in kindergarten is learned primarily through the world of the classroom and places that can be visited, such as the post office, fire station, zoo, or pond. Parents who assist on class trips should dress comfortably. Kindergarten trips aren't like grown-up trips. Kindergarten experiences are active, sometimes even messy. Teachers often tell parents, "Please, don't send your child to school in party clothes. Dress them for paint, paste, and being outdoors."

Places children can't visit can be taught through pictures and video, but less effectively. Thus, city children learning about farms without ever seeing a garden is somewhat of a waste of time, as is country children studying skyscrapers and subways through pictures. The main purpose of trips in kindergarten is to broaden children's understanding of people and the ways they live together. Parents visiting classrooms to tell about their jobs is a way of

teaching social studies, especially if the parents bring in tools and work uni-forms—things the children can *touch*.

In social studies children learn about themselves, both how they are unique and how they are part of a group. Sharing, cooperating, planning, leading, responsibility, deciding upon rules, and following rules are practiced over and over throughout the school year. These are not innate skills but skills that are acquired in a slow process during the growing years. Next to the family, the school is the most important influence on a child's character. What schools do to encourage positive social behavior is crucial to society at large and not measurable by academic tests.

Kindergarten teachers have classroom rules that are stated clearly in positive ways so that they make sense to children. Instead of saying, "Don't run," early childhood teachers say, "We walk in the halls so that we stay together and so that we don't trip and fall." Kindergarten teachers maintain calm in the classroom so that the children can talk and listen to each other. Productive kindergarten classrooms are neither rigid with stillness nor frantic with noise.

Art

Kindergarten teachers provide art materials that are accessible to children because young children like to do things for themselves. They like to express themselves and record their ideas with clay, paper, crayons, markers, paint, paste, and collage materials.

What's the point of the art project if they all turn out the same? Some-times the point is to show children techniques, such as leaf rubbing, which is

Let's put the wet boots here...

fine. And sometimes the point is to get kids to listen and follow directions, and that's fine too. But most of the time, children should be given the freedom to use their imaginations. Rather than being told how to make a turkey, they should be asked: How could you make a turkey? Or a monster? Or a spaceship? Or a magic egg in which you could live if you were a magic bird?

Music

It used to be that most kindergarten teachers played the piano, guitar, or autoharp; nowadays, fewer teachers have these skills, an unfortunate development that hopefully will improve, for children respond well to music. They love to sing and enact musical fantasies. Musical activities give children another medium for expressing themselves and sharing ideas with others.

In the new kindergarten, teachers who do not know how to play instruments provide music for their children using the excellent records by Ella Jenkins, Tom Glazer, Hap Palmer, Raffi, and others. Such records can be found in catalogs from companies such as Childcraft Education Corporation in Edison, New Jersey. (For the complete address, see the Appendix.)

Using rhythm instruments, such as drums, bells, triangles, and shakers, children are helped to reproduce rhythms they hear and invent new rhythms for others to copy. It takes special talent and time to unfold young children's musical abilities, but the results are satisfying because music means so much to them.

Through musical shows children plan and practice together for parents, children gain in confidence and camaraderie. Often, such shows encourage parental involvement in comfortable ways that draw parents closer to an understanding of the overall kindergarten curriculum.

Can you make this sound? DING! DING!

Physical Education

Young children are always being physically educated. Their bodies are growing rapidly, and they are constantly moving about. Just watch a group of kindergartners sitting on a rug in a classroom listening to a story being read aloud. They fidget and change positions. Even afterward, when they talk about the story, they move their hands, arms, and heads.

Physical education for young children focuses on movement in order to help children strengthen their muscles and coordinate actions. Recess does this too, but a special physical education program can focus on specific activities that supplement classroom learning: listening, following directions, knowing the difference between left and right, balancing, and moving to music.

In some districts where kindergartens are part of an elementary school, kindergartners go to the school gym for instruction several times a week. To do so, they may pass through the rest of the school, which in itself is a social studies trip that is fascinating to five-year-olds.

In the new kindergarten physical education teachers and kindergarten teachers plan together ahead of time to assure that the program is appropriate for the children and wherever possible related to themes being explored in the classroom. Sometimes they plan special movement activities involving music that supplements a special topic, such as wind, volcanoes, animals, or plants.

I CAN REACH UP TO THE SKY...

Chapter Three

How to Organize and Manage a Full-Day, Child-Centered, Academic Kindergarten

As the noted Swiss educational psychologist Jean Piaget stressed, autonomy is an important factor in children's learning. When children are able to discover answers for themselves, they learn more effectively than when they are told answers by a teacher. The best kindergarten classrooms are managed so that children can direct their own learning as much as possible.

A classroom in which children are encouraged to direct their own learning is often called a child-centered classroom. The child-centered classroom is set up with centers, special areas of investigation that children visit at different times during the day. Some of the most popular centers are: the reading or library center, the listening center (where children listen to tapes and records through earphones), the writing center, the science center, the math center (often combined with the science center), the game center (equipped with various educational games and puzzles), the block center, the housekeeping or family living center, the art center, and the water/sand table center. Other centers might be the show and tell center (where children display items they have brought to class), the music center, the quiet center, and the puppet stage. A list of sources of materials for centers can be found in the Appendix.

Centers are arranged to accommodate several children at a time. Teach-

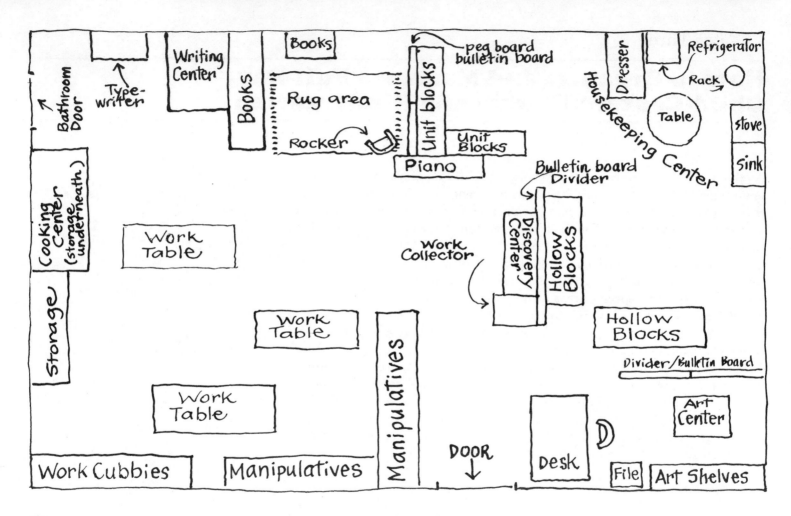

26

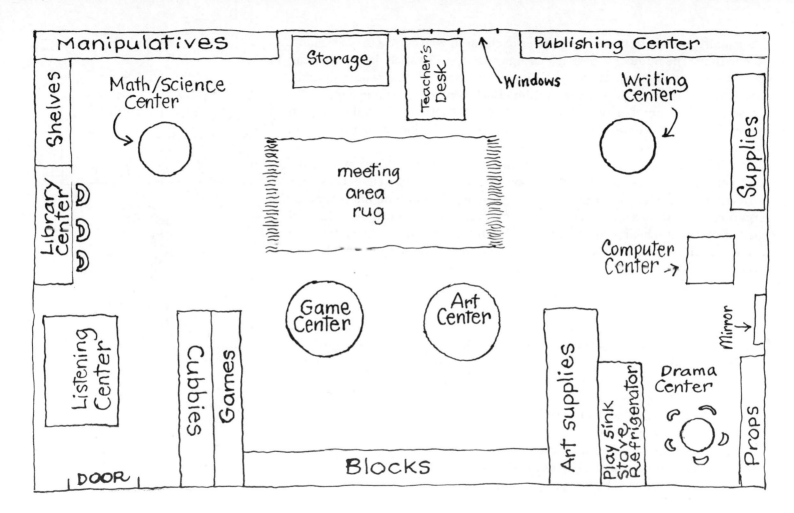

ers usually place a limit on the number of children who can be in each center at one time. The number is posted on a sign that also has stick figures showing how many are allowed, and/or the number of chairs in the center signifies how many children can be in the center. Each center is given enough space for the allotted number of children to function effectively. In order to have sufficiently roomy centers, teachers may have to limit the number of centers in classrooms or redo centers from time to time.

Managing the flow of children in and out of centers and overseeing the instruction that goes on in them is one of the most basic challenges of a kindergarten teacher. In order to do the job, she needs to combine pragmatic organization with an understanding of children and the purpose of kindergarten. Without a hearty blend of planning *and* theory, kindergarten teachers are ineffective; when this happens, they have to step back and rethink their program.

Schedules

Only after children's needs are identified and program goals established are teachers able to go ahead and create a practical daily schedule for coordinating children, materials, space, and time. Because teachers and classes are different, no one schedule works for every school. A good teacher finds a way to manage her classroom that works for her and the children. Once she finds such a schedule, she does not carve it in stone, but rather she adapts it and improves it as she goes along.

Being able to make a classroom "work" is an accomplishment, and teachers who can do it feel understandably proud of their work. It is helpful for teachers to share scheduling ideas with each other, especially as they

discover new ideas and identify additional needs of children. Parents like to see a copy of their children's schedule. They appreciate having a sense of their children's days so they can picture them at school and so they can talk with their child more vividly about school at the end of the day.

A good teacher has both long-range and short-range plans. Long-range plans may encompass a plan of themes to be covered during the year. In this book ten themes are presented and suggested for ten months of the year, but teachers should feel free to use themes of their own choice in whatever order suits them. The advantage of a monthly theme is that it pulls the content of a program together so that children's interest can flow meaningfully from one activity to another.

Teaching Children the Schedule

Short-term plans are plans for the week or day. In the beginning of the school year, kindergarten teachers plan time to teach children the daily operation of the classroom. Each activity of the day is presented clearly, with expected behaviors modeled by the teacher so the children know what to do. What to do with your coat and lunch box, what may be done during free play, how to assemble for circle time, how to walk in the hallway, how to use the bathrooms, how to use tempera paints, how to use various learning centers, how to put away materials, and so forth—the teacher takes plenty of time in the first weeks of school to show and explain these activities to children so that they know how to behave. Taking sufficient time to teach children how to be kindergartners pays off for the rest of the year because it enables children to acquire a sense of control over themselves and their environment. They like to know what is expected of them.

THIS IS HOW WE LINE UP TO GO HOME EVERY DAY.

Discipline

A key factor to the success of a child-centered classroom is teaching children at the beginning of the school year how to work and play independently.

Establishing a mood of autonomy, inquiry, sharing, and respect in the classroom enables children to feel pride in their ideas and to be curious about the ideas of others. Such a classroom atmosphere leads to improvement in the children's ability to listen to each other and to focus on their own activities without being distracted. The new kindergarten is quiet with the hum of activity; it is a pleasant place to be.

Discipline in the new kindergarten is based on positive reasons for respecting each other and being safe. Teachers state rules in a way that helps children understand them: We take turns in centers so that they don't get crowded; we walk so we don't fall down; in a group discussion we raise our hands so each of us can be called on and heard by everyone else; we share materials so that we each get a chance to use them; we clean up after ourselves so that the next person has a place to play.

Because young children can get rambunctious, they need clear signals to tell them when to calm down. Teachers teach the signals at the beginning of the year. "When I feel you're getting too noisy, I'll turn the lights off and on two times. That will be a special signal for you to quiet down." Or, "When I clap my hands three times, please stop what you are doing and listen to me because that will be a signal that I have a special announcement to make." Or, "When I ring my bell, that is a signal to clean up and get ready for lunch." Or, "When I start to sing a certain song, that is a signal to meet on the rug for circle time." Children enjoy learning the meaning of special signals and enjoy being able to act in accordance with them.

We raise our hands and speak one at a time, so we'll be able to hear each other's ideas.

Good teachers know that you don't just tell children to get ready for lunch, you teach them at the beginning of the year exactly what "getting ready for lunch" means in your classroom: putting away equipment, getting in line, washing hands, and so forth. Sometimes teachers invite children to give their ideas for improving classroom procedures.

In the new kindergarten thinking skills are stressed, not just in science and math, but in all aspects of the day. The children become used to the teacher asking them how to solve all different kinds of problems. When a problem of discipline arises, children are asked to think how to solve it. For example, if two children are fighting over a toy, the teacher can ask for the toy and say, "How can you solve the problem you two have? You both want the toy. What can you two do about that?" The teacher might put the toy away until the children solve the problem.

What can you do to solve your problem?

An Atmosphere of Learning

A sense of inquiry pervades the new kindergarten. Children learn to explore materials, make predictions, test predictions, come to their own conclusions, record their ideas, and share them with others. In time, the process of inquiry becomes second nature to the children, who soon become able to manage the stages themselves with little help from their teacher. The teacher is now free to visit centers and teach. As children learn, she supports them and leads them to further discovery with open-ended questions and support. By respecting children's autonomy, she helps children feel pride in themselves as excellent learners.

What to Do Where

In a child-centered classroom teaching methods and physical environment go together hand in hand. In the centers, teachers help children explore materials individually or in small groups. There is usually a special area in the room where the class can meet as a whole. Often, this meeting takes place in a circle and/or on a rug on which everyone can sit comfortably; hence, meeting time may be called "circle time" or "rug time." Sometimes the whole class may need to sit at tables to do a class activity. If the tables are in centers, the children can sit there, or the tables can be moved together in the center of the room.

   The activities in this book are written to involve action on the part of children. Where they are best done in the classroom depends on the teacher, the children, the classroom setup, and perhaps the presence of a teacher aide. Teachers are invited to use their own judgment in adapting the ideas in this book to their specific setups. If the ideas are adapted to centers (and it is hoped that many of them will be), teachers need to demonstrate to the children exactly what task they are expected to do at the center. Often, the task is presented as a question to explore in the center, such as: "How many beans do you think are in this jar? The jar will be in the math center this week. When you go to that center, look at the jar. Estimate and record your answer on a slip of paper along with your name. Put your answer in the red box. You may also play with other materials in the math center. On Thursday we will make a graph of our estimates. On Friday we will count the beans."

   As much as possible, have children in centers record their discoveries in concrete ways: by writing, drawing, making models, doing a ditto, or mark-

ing a graph. This way, it is easier to share and keep track of children's accomplishments.

Children and parents may enjoy being involved in helping to think up tasks for centers. Asking parents to help in such a way enables them to understand better how centers promote classroom learning.

Children in a child-centered classroom rotate jobs that keep their classroom organized and functioning. Their jobs might be: center checker, line leader, door holder, snack helper, table setter, table clearer, floor cleaner, and paintbrush washer. Teachers have job charts on the wall with pictures and names of each job and a system for rotating children's names. In some places the children's names are written on tags that are hung up under the job pictures. Or children's names are written on clothespins and clipped to the job pictures. The children enjoy their jobs because they give them a sense of helping to run their classroom.

Because classrooms vary in size and equipment, it is difficult to present one ideal classroom arrangement and schedule that works for everyone. Teachers have to arrange their classrooms and plan their schedules in ways that best suit their children's needs and kindergarten's goals. However, here are some sample schedules and classroom arrangements to stimulate thought and ideas.

My job for the week is sweeper.

Kindergarten Schedule 1

8:40 – 8:50	Children arrive
8:50 – 9:10	Meeting (attendance, pledge, song, calendar, weather)
9:10 – 11:00	Language Arts/ Centers
11:00 – 11:25	Recess
11:25 – 11:55	Lunch
11:55 – 12:10	Quiet Time
12:10 – 12:30	Story Time (Each week a different author is featured.)
12:30 – 1:00	Math
1:00 – 2:30	Science, Social Studies, Special Projects, Centers
2:30 – 2:45	Show and Tell
2:45 – 2:55	Clean Up, Jobs, Ready to Go
2:55 – 3:00	Dismissal

Kindergarten Schedule 2

8:30 – 9:00	Meeting Time
9:00 – 10:00	Language Arts
10:00 – 10:15	Exercises and Music
10:15 – 10:30	Rest Rooms/Snack
10:30 – 11:00	Math
11:00 – 11:20	Recess/P.E./ Environmental Studies
11:20 – 12:00	Learning Centers
12:00 – 12:10	Rest Rooms
12:10 – 12:30	Lunch
12:30 – 12:45	Story Time
12:45 – 1:30	Rest and Relaxation
1:30 – 2:00	Recess/P.E./ Environmental Studies
2:00 – 2:15	Rest Rooms/Snack
2:15 – 2:45	Arts and Crafts/ Social Studies/ Science
2:45 – 3:00	Prepare to Go Home
3:00 – 3:15	Dismissal/Parent Conferences

Kindergarten Schedule 3

8:30 – 9:00	Circle Time/ Calendar
9:00 – 10:00	Language Arts
10:00 – 10:30	Centers
10:30 – 10:45	Recess
10:45 – 11:15	Social Studies
11:15 – 12:00	Art
12:00 – 12:40	Lunch
12:40 – 1:40	Lunch & Independent Play
1:40 – 2:10	P.E./Music
2:10 – 2:40	Math/Science
2:40 – 3:00	Jobs, Clean Up, Get Ready to Go Home

Managing the Day: Kindergarten 1

The following description is of a day in kindergarten #1 on page 34. Bear in mind that it reflects a typical day in the middle of the school year; in other words, children have already been trained how to operate in the classroom.

Monday is an important day. On this day, centers and jobs change. At the morning meeting (which is extra-long on Mondays), children learn of their new jobs for the week and see their names on a rebus job chart. (The rebus chart shows pictures for the various jobs.) Certain children are appointed center leaders. The center leaders take turns and go to their centers and bring whatever is new back to the meeting area. The teacher goes over the new item with the children, teaching them what to do with it, and posing questions and tasks for them to do with it when they get to the center. The listening center leader, for example, shows the other children the new tape or record that the children will hear that week. In many classrooms one author is studied per week, so the introduction of the new tape is an opportunity to introduce the new author too and show some of the author's books.

Each center leader is given a chart with every child's name on it. The center leaders tape the charts to a table in their centers. As children use the center, they cross out their name on the chart. The center leaders keep track of who hasn't been to the center. On Thursdays and Fridays they remind classmates to catch up. At the end of each center period, center leaders check to see that their centers are cleaned up properly.

At the beginning of the year children are assigned to centers, where they must stay for fifteen to twenty minutes before being reassigned to other centers. As the year progresses, children do not need to be assigned. They are allowed to choose centers, as long as they do not exceed the number allowed in each center. They may move on to other centers as they please. During the week, however, they must visit every center, or especially centers that are "must do" centers.

If a center is not popular, something's wrong with it. Either the task is not clear, or it's too hard, or it's boring. Teachers should revamp unpopular centers. The children should be given a sense that, while center work is serious, it should also be fun.

Sometimes, while children are at centers, teachers or aides pull a small group of children together for special small-group instruction, often involving writing and reading activities. The teacher may have a special table near her desk for this purpose.

Sometimes, while children are at centers, teachers visit them there, participating in and strengthening the learning that's going on. Often, the centers are where the most exciting moments of learning occur. And they are where the best opportunities occur for teachers to observe and evaluate children's strengths and weaknesses.

Evaluation

I have not yet seen a kindergarten report card that reflects accurately the learning that goes on in a child-centered, academic classroom, but hopefully one will be developed someday. In order to be effective, it will have to reflect the depth of children's learning and the sophistication of the processes they are using (such as graphing amounts, recording ideas, using the scientific method, operating independently, brainstorming, critical thinking, sharing discoveries with each other) as well as the specific tasks they are mastering (such as writing on their own level, reading their writing, number recognition,

letter recognition, and so forth). Furthermore, no written test thus far developed seems to be able to diagnose fully children's real learning needs and strengths, though some checklists can be used to keep track of certain skills, such as ability to tie one's shoes, ability to identify letter sounds, and ability to hear rhyming words. Teachers may want to make up their own checklists/report cards that reflect their own programs.

Thus, so far, at the kindergarten level the best evaluations of children are anecdotal. Teachers can keep notebooks with a page for each child in which to record thoughts and observations. These anecdotes can be shared with parents, and parents can be encouraged to contribute ideas of their own.

Diagnosing Special Needs

Any special learning problems should be discussed with parents and referred to special education teachers. Kindergarten teachers usually are quite good at spotting eye and ear problems that parents might not notice at home because they are so used to their children.

Parent Communication

An important aspect of the new kindergarten is parent communication. Teachers use many different methods to involve parents in the program. Parent newsletters tell about student activities in the classroom and invite parents to visit the classroom. Parents Night provides an opportunity for parents to see how a child-centered classroom really works. Many teachers actually have the parents visit centers and do tasks so that they can see what autonomous learning can produce.

Parents and grandparents are invited to celebrate special occasions at the school, such as a Thanksgiving feast, a holiday sing-along, and Grandparents' Day. Parents are invited to contribute materials to the classroom and to share special skills and hobbies they have. Parents volunteer to help on class trips, and class "mothers" or "fathers" help to arrange events, making important telephone calls to class parents.

One of the most important payoffs of involving parents meaningfully in a child-centered, academic kindergarten is that parents come to see for themselves that children learn best not through abstract paper-and-pencil drill-type activities, but through active, concrete, self-motivated investigation. Parent involvement is parent training, and parents who have been trained through class involvement are better able to help their children learn at home.

The next ten chapters of *The New Kindergarten* present ten different themes for investigation in the classroom. As teachers cover a theme in the classroom, they usually send a note home to parents explaining about it, describing what children will learn, and suggesting ways parents might become involved. At the beginning of the year teachers can announce the themes for the year ahead of time so that parents have plenty of time to plan how they might participate.

Chapter Four

Theme: The Child and the Five Senses

A good month in which to explore the theme of the child and the five senses is September or the first month of the school year. The goal of the unit is to instill children with a sense of identity and self-worth. Because it is the beginning of the school year, a secondary goal is to help the child acclimate to classmates and school activities. The topic of the five senses provides opportunities to talk about one's self and all that one can experience in the immediate environment: shapes, colors, and basic school equipment such as paints, puzzles, puppets, and blocks.

The theme can be revisited in June or the last month of the school year as a way of recording children's growth and progress. Many of the projects can then be repeated and compared with those saved from the beginning of the year.

Language Arts: Oral Language

Reciting chants together provides children with opportunity to practice verbal skills, experience rhythm, and feel the satisfaction of saying rhymes in unison. Use chants at various times of day to promote a feeling of group togetherness. Pass-along chants can be changed by the children as they are passed along in a circle.

Skooby Doo Names Chant

Today is ———— . (day of week)
Skooby doo.
I am ———— . (child's name)
Who are you?

Pass this chant around a circle having each child say a verse. Clap while you say the chant, stopping to hear the individual names.

Fiddle-I-Fo Choosing Chant

Fiddle-I-Fo, Fiddle-I-Fee,
———— is(are) what I choose for me.

Use this chant when you want children to select jobs, games, or activities; or use it in games to have them select colors, shapes, or toys they like. Choices can be graphed in a follow-up math activity. To make a graph, see page 50.

Fiddle-I-Fo, Fiddle-I-Fee,
Red is what I choose for me!

Language Arts: Listening

Rhyming Game

This game can instigate an ongoing project set up in the listening center. The idea is to collect real things or small models of things that rhyme. Children and their parents can contribute to the game at any time. (Parents can have fun with this.) Store the collection in a special box labeled RHYMING GAME. (Perhaps you can decorate it with rhyming pictures.) To play the game, children sort objects into rhyming pairs. Plastic charms and tiny miniatures make great rhyming objects.

Recommended Read-Aloud Books

☐ *The Wonderful Shrinking Shirt,* Anderson (Albert Whitman)—story of a shirt that shrinks.

☐ *Curious George,* Rey (Houghton Mifflin)—another troublemaker children can identify with.

☐ *When I Was Young in the Mountains,* Rylant (Dutton)—lovely rendition of the life of a southern mountain girl long ago.

☐ *Tell Me a Mitzi,* Segal (Farrar)—funny story of a New York City girl.

☐ *The Story of Ferdinand,* Leaf (Viking)—wonderful story of a peace-loving bull.

☐ *Frederick,* Lionni (Pantheon)—story about a charming mouse poet.

☐ *The Growing Story,* Kraus (Harper)—A farm boy's clothes from last year no longer fit.

☐ *Is It Red? Is It Yellow? Is It Blue?* and *Round & Round & Round* and *Is It Rough? Is It Smooth? Is It Shiny?* Hoban (Greenwillow)—three beautiful books of photographs showing things that can be perceived with the five senses.

Language Arts: Writing

Class Scrapbook

Ask the children to draw self-portraits. Put the self-portraits in a scrapbook on the right-hand pages. On the left-hand pages write, or let the children write, their names. "Read" the class scrapbook together from time to time. Store it with other classroom books for the children to look at when they want.

At the end of the year, make another class scrapbook. Compare portraits, noting how they are similar and how they are different. Share the beginning-of-the-year and end-of-the-year portraits with parents so they can see how their children have grown and changed.

September

June

Language Arts: Reading

Letters and Words Around Us

Make your classroom an environment in which letters and words play an important, comfortable part. Here are some ways to do this:

1. Have a big alphabet chart on the wall where children see it easily.

2. Put cuddly alphabet pillows in the reading center. Perhaps parents could volunteer to make them.

3. Label important classroom objects. Let the children see you doing this.

4. Put alphabet toys that are fun to play with in the game center and the reading center.

5. Have plenty of books accessible for the children to look at. Read picture books often to the children.

6. Have an experience chart handy for recording children's words so you can read them back to them afterward.

Social Studies

Photo Puppets and Puppet Theater

Take a close-up photograph of each child's face. Help the children paste the photographs on tongue depressors to make puppets. When the photos are dry, help the children strengthen the connection between the photo and the stick with tape. Write the name of each child in marker on the stick.

Store the photo puppets in a convenient place so that the children can use them for dramatic play. You may find that they come in handy to solve social problems in the classroom. For example, if two children are fighting, you can have their puppets talk to each other about the problem. Let children give ideas for what the puppets could say to each other.

Make a puppet theater from a washing machine box. Cut the doors and windows out with a serrated knife or saw. Only the teacher should do this, but the children can watch and later paint the theater.

Social Studies

Eye Doctors and Ear Doctors

CONCEPT: *Nurses and doctors can test our eyes and ears. If we need to, we can get glasses and hearing aids to help us see and hear better. Eye doctors and ear doctors specialize in eyes and ears.*

Invite the nurse or whoever tests children's eyes and ears to class to explain the kinds of tests she or he uses. Use the experience to help the children develop vocabulary words for describing sounds: *high/low, loud/soft.* Show them an eye chart so that they will know what the eye test is like. Explain that eye and ear tests can be fun to take. Encourage the children to ask questions about the nurse's or doctor's job. Afterward, write a class thank-you letter to the visitor.

47

Science

Sense of Taste

What words do we have to describe tastes? *Sweet, sour, salty.* Give the children different foods to taste: salted crackers and potato chips (for salty), grapes and raisins (for sweet), lemon slices and sour pickles (for sour).

Taste different kinds of apples. Which apples are sweet? Which apples are sour?

What foods taste good with apples? (Try peanut butter spread on slices, cheese slices on apple slices, cottage cheese and chopped apples, yogurt and chopped apples.) Record the favorite combinations on an experience chart.

Sense of Hearing

Ask each child for "homework" to bring in something that makes a noise. (It can be as elaborate as a toy musical instrument or as simple as a rattle made by putting pebbles in an empty, clean margarine tub.) Ask them to keep their noisemakers a surprise by bringing them inside a bag or their lunch boxes.

One by one, ask the children to share their noisemakers with the class in a way that the noisemaker cannot be seen. Ask the other children to guess what the noisemaker is.

Sense of Smell

Have the children take turns wearing blindfolds or closing their eyes tightly while you or other children give them interesting things to identify by smell. Try *bananas, peanut butter, lemon, oranges, a candy cane, and coconut.*

Science

Sense of Sight and Sense of Touch

A sand and water play table gives children the opportunity to learn firsthand about the senses of sight and touch, as well as the opportunity to use these senses to develop critical thinking abilities and familiarity with the scientific process. Over and over, as children play at the sand and water table, they make predictions, carry out experiments, and discover results. Help them record their results on worksheets designed to suit their sand and water play activities.

Math

Sorting, Counting, and Graphing Ourselves

CONCEPT: *People have different color eyes. We can sort ourselves into groups based on eye color.*

Have the children sort themselves into groups based on eye color. Then let each group pick the color construction paper that matches their eyes and cut out eyes from it. If they like, they can trace eye patterns and afterward color their eyes with crayons or markers.

To record the groups, have the children paste their eyes on a graph, starting at the bottom and building up. Explain that a graph is a picture of "how many." Count how many there are of each eye color. Compare the amounts in the various groups. Ask "Which eye color do we have the most of? Fewest of?" As you work on the graph, help the children develop vocabulary: *more, most, least, fewest, some, none,* and so forth.

Make other graphs that tell about the children in the class, such as graphs that show hair color, shoe color, and how children come to school.

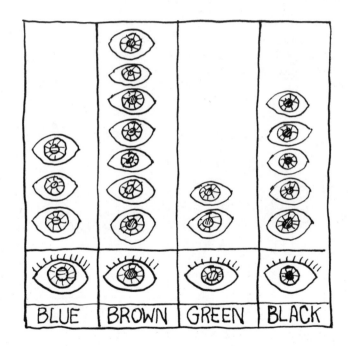

Math

Measuring Ourselves

Trace the children on butcher paper, and have them color their self-portraits. Give them one-foot-long shoe patterns to trace and paste next to their portraits to measure how many feet tall they are.

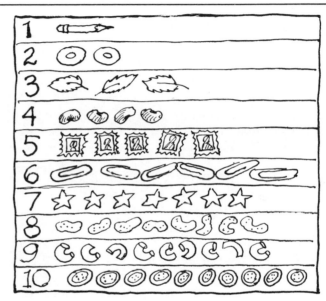

Number Charts

Give each child a piece of experience chart paper. Write, or have the child write, numbers 1 to 10 going down the left-hand side. Give the children small objects to paste next to each number. Ask to check their amounts before they paste them down.

51

Art

Shapes and Colors Treasure Hunt

Give the children oaktag patterns of circles, squares, rectangles, and triangles to trace and cut out of colored paper. Help them identify and discuss the shapes and colors as they work. Put the cutout shapes in a shopping bag and call it The Treasure Hunt Bag. Ask each child to pick three shapes from the bag and then try to find three things in the classroom to match the shapes. For example, a child with a red circle, blue triangle, and green rectangle might find a red ball, a blue sail, and a green book. Have the children share their treasures with each other, then put them back. Afterward, have them draw or paint pictures of treasures they found or treasures they would like to find. The paintings do not have to be of particular shapes or colors. Let the children feel free to paint whatever they like.

Art

Play Dough Shape Pictures and Color Mixing

Help the children make play dough by mixing 2 cups flour, 3/4 cup salt, 1 tablespoon salad oil, and 1/2 cup water. If the dough is too sticky, add flour or salt. If it is too dry, add water. Knead well. Give each child a ball to play with.

TO MAKE PLAY DOUGH SHAPE PICTURES: Roll out or press the play dough flat with your hand. Imprint it with shapes found in the classroom to make a shaped design. Try making a pattern from the shapes. See if a friend can copy your pattern.

TO MIX COLORS: Divide your play dough ball into three smaller balls. Add red food coloring to one, blue food coloring to another, and yellow food coloring to the third. Knead the balls separately to mix the color into the ball. Then try different color mixing experiments. Ask "What happens if you mix a piece of yellow play dough with a piece of red play dough? What color do you get?" Have the children record their answers with crayons on paper. Teach them the meaning of the symbols + ("and") and = ("make") so they can read their results back afterward.

PAPER PLATE   DOUGH

53

Music

Body Parts Songs

Review body parts by singing songs about them. Touch or shake the body parts as you name them, turning the songs into exercise songs, if you like.

This Old Man

This old man, he played one,
He played knick knack on his thumb,
With a knick knack paddy whack,
Give a dog a bone,
This old man came rolling home.

Two . . . shoe,
Three . . . knee,
Four . . . floor,
Five . . . side,
Six . . . hips,
Seven . . . up to heaven,
Eight . . . on his pate,*
Nine . . . on his spine,
Ten . . . once again.

*Top of head.

Head, Shoulders, Knees, and Toes

(to the tune of "There Is a Tavern in the Town"

Head, shoulders, knees, and toes,
Knees and toes.
Head, shoulders, knees, and toes,
Knees and toes-s and—
Eyes and ears
And mouth and nose,
Head, shoulders, knees, and toes,
Knees and toes.

Music

Five Senses Song

Where Is Round Shape?

(Played similarly to "Where Is Thumbkin" and sung to the tune of "Frère Jacques")

Have the children sit in a circle with different shapes held in their hands behind them. Sing the song, calling out different shapes for them to identify with their hands and show as they sing the lines, "Here I am./Here I am."

VARIATIONS: Give the children different textures or objects to feel and identify.

Where is round shape?
Where is round shape?
Here I am.
Here I am.
How are you today, sir? (ma'am?)
Very fine and thank you.
Run away.
Run away.

Recommended Records

☐ *Songs About Me* and *More Songs About Me* by William Janiak (Kimbo).

Physical Education

Listening Game

Everyone sits in a big circle. In the middle of the circle sits IT on a chair. Under the chair is an object such as a toy car or a block. IT is blindfolded or has eyes closed tightly. The teacher points to one person in the circle. That person creeps toward the chair, occasionally making a tiny, quiet noise like *beep, beep*. IT listens and tries to tag the beeper/creeper—without moving off the chair. If IT tags the person, that person becomes the next IT. If the beeper/creeper can grab the object under the chair and go back to the circle without being tagged, he or she appoints the next beeper/creeper, and IT remains on the chair.

HINT: This is a nice, quiet game for a rainy day.

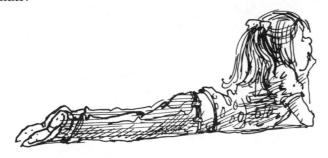

Physical Education

Simon Says

At first, the teacher is Simon and faces the children, who stand spread out in a roomy space indoors or out. Each child should be able to swing his or her arms around without hitting another child, and each child should be able to see Simon well. Simon gives commands for the children to follow, such as "Simon says, 'Swing your arms in the air,'" or "Simon says, 'Kick your feet.'" The children are to obey only those commands that begin with the words "Simon says." If the command does not begin with these words (for example, "Stamp your feet"), the players should ignore it. Play the game noncompetitively. Each time a child makes a mistake, enjoy a good laugh together with the child, but do not send the child out of the game.

5

Chapter 5

Theme: Home and Community

A good month in which to explore the theme of home and community is October for several reasons: (1) Fire Prevention Week is during October and fire fighters, interesting community workers, are usually prepared for visits from children; (2) Halloween provides an opportunity to discuss costumes, dressing up like community workers, and fire safety; and (3) the study of home and community leads naturally from the study of the child. Traditionally, the sequence of topics in the kindergarten school year has gone from the child to the family to the home and to the community. However, in past years many people have come to feel that the topic of families is too private for classroom study. Home as a topic is better because it encompasses families and the kinds of places families live. The goal of a unit on home and community together is to instill children with a sense that they are cared for in special ways and by special people both in their homes and in their community.

Language Arts: Oral Language

Community Workers and Props for Dramatic Play

CONCEPTS: *Community workers help people in a community. A community is where you live and the people who live there with you. You can pretend you are community workers.*

Help children learn about community workers who are visible in your area. Try to visit workers at their place of work, or invite workers to visit your class. Prepare questions ahead of time on an experience chart. Encourage the children to ask why workers use particular clothes and equipment. Afterward, introduce appropriate props for dramatic play in the housekeeping corner.

- Fire Fighter's Props: *fire hat, raincoat, boots, toy fire trucks, walkie-talkie*
- Postal Worker's Props: *envelopes, stickers, stamps and stamp pads, mailboxes, toy mail trucks*
- Nurse's and Doctor's Props: *gauze, bandages, a real stethoscope, small plastic bottles, cotton balls*
- Teacher's Props: *paper, pencils, crayons, experience chart, small blackboard, chalk*
- Storekeeper's Props: *toy cash register, play money, large blank price tags, pretend food, empty food containers and boxes, toy shopping cart*

- Cook's Props: *pots, pans, bowls, cooking and eating utensils, plates, cups, play stove, sink, refrigerator*
- Police Officer's Props: *police officer's cap, walkie-talkie, whistle, pad and pencil, toy gun*
- Pumpkin Farmer's Props: *overalls, straw hat, real pumpkins* (Use the pumpkins for dramatic play for a day, then use them in the math center. Ask the children to predict how many seeds are in each pumpkin. Cut the pumpkins open and count to see who came closest.) More pumpkin activities: (1) roast the pumpkin seeds (see page 84); (2) draw pumpkin faces on orange paper; (3) carve (the teacher does this) a jack-o'-lantern to match it.

I am a farmer. I grow pumpkins and sell them to kids for Jack-O'-lanterns.

Language Arts: Listening

Masks

Ask the children, "What do you want to be when you grow up?" Show them how to make paper-bag masks to express their ideas, drawing faces on the bags with markers and crayons. Provide patterns for caps that they can trace, cut out, and paste on their masks, if they like. Provide yarn for hair and beards and cloth for clothes. After the masks are finished, ask the children to put them on and tell about themselves as grown-ups. Encourage the children to listen carefully to each other.

To make masks comfortable for children to wear: (1) Tear foldlines partway so the mask fits on the child comfortably. (2) Teacher: cut eyeholes so the child can see. The cut eyeholes do not have to be where the drawn eyes are.

Recommended Read-Aloud Books

- [ ] *The Pain and the Great One*, Blume (Bradbury)—sibling rivalry exposed humorously.
- [ ] *Red Sun Girl*, Marzollo (Dial)—A girl who's different from her family gets help from the wise fox woman.
- [ ] *Mo to the Rescue*, Osborne (Dial)—A good-natured sheriff protects his animal community.
- [ ] *The Park Book*, Zolotow (Harper)—a friendly account of city park life.
- [ ] *Building a House*, Barton (Greenwillow)—a simplified account with clear pictures.
- [ ] *Buffalo Woman*, Goble (Bradbury)—a Great Plains Native American legend about a girl who must pass tests to join the buffalo nation.
- [ ] *Make Way for Ducklings*, McCloskey (Viking)—Mother and Father Mallard find a home for their family in Boston.
- [ ] *Six Chinese Brothers*, Hou-tien (Holt)—Six clever brothers rescue their father.
- [ ] *The Little Fireman*, Brown (Addison-Wesley)—a wonderful story about a little fireman and a big fireman.

Language Arts: Writing

A Visit to the Fire Station

To help the children prepare for a visit to the fire station, ask them to brainstorm a list of things they expect to see at the fire station. Write the list on an experience chart, illustrating each item with a picture. Bring the pad and list with you to the fire station. Check off the things as you see them. Make a new list of other things you saw.

After your trip, write a class thank-you letter to the fire fighters. Write the letter the children dictate on an experience chart. Have the children sign their names in different colors, however they write them. Writing their names in different colors will help children find their names to read back afterward.

Language Arts: Reading

Stories About Families and Homes

Many people feel that it is an invasion of children's privacy to ask them to tell about their families in school, and indeed it may be trying for a particular child with family problems to talk about his or her family in school. Yet, families are important, as children well know. One way to talk about families in school is to talk about the families we meet through children's literature.

As you read books about families to children (see page 61), elicit through class discussion the following concepts: *Families are the same in many ways.* (Ask children to tell you how families in stories are the same.) *Families are also different in many ways.* (Ask children to tell you how families in stories are different.)

In class you might want the children to make up stories about imaginary families. Perhaps the children can act them out with puppets. Children who want to tell stories about their own real families are, of course, welcome to do so. Stories can be told aloud, through pictures, through words dictated to a grown-up or into a tape recorder, or through dramatic play, especially in the housekeeping corner.

Social Studies

Block Play

Blocks can be used to stimulate children's thinking in different ways. Children can use them to make homes, hospitals, bridges, tunnels, barns, castles, airports, and skyscrapers. Some of the structures children make in the block corner may be representations of buildings they are familiar with such as the school and local gas station. The children use the blocks to show what they already know about these places. With blocks they can map out places they have been.

Often children use blocks to build imaginary structures, such as castles and elaborate tunnels. Often they proceed happily and busily without needing help from you, but you may be able to enhance their creativity with questions such as, "Where do the king and queen eat?" or "What kind of building could you make that would be different or the opposite from this building?"

Another way to inspire thoughtful block building in the classroom is to display photographs of real buildings and challenge the children, "Can you build a building like this? What would you need to do it? How would you go about doing it?" Record the children's answers on a tape recorder or an experience chart.

Social Studies

Halloween Safety Posters

Discuss Halloween safety rules with the children, asking them to tell you the rules and why they are important. Elicit a list of rules like the following. Try to state the rules in positive, not negative, ways. Ask the children to select rules and make paintings to illustrate them. Afterward, display the paintings and review the safety rules. If you like, write the rules on the paintings and send some to a local newspaper for possible publication at Halloween time.

Safety rules to discuss:

- Go trick-or-treating with a grown-up.
- Walk. Don't run.
- Wear bright clothes.
- Watch out for cars.
- Stay away from lit jack-o'-lanterns.
- If you wear a mask, make sure you can see well.
- Bring your trick-or-treat foods home; then only eat what your parents say you may eat.

Science

Time Lines

The concept of time is difficult for young children for whom "long ago" seems like yesterday and "tomorrow" the far distant future. To help children with the idea of time, set up a display area with lines connecting pictures that show the progression of time. Encourage children to bring in or draw pictures that show how things change with time. Use the pictures to teach the vocabulary words *long ago, now; before, after; first, next; then, finally.*

People change.

Trees change.

Buildings change.

Science

Autumn Leaves

CONCEPT: *We have different kinds of trees in our community.*

Collect leaves on a nature walk in the school yard or park. Bring them back to class and ask, "How many ways can we sort these leaves?" Encourage the children to think of different, interesting ways to sort them, such as by color, by shape, by conditions (perfect specimens and imperfect ones), by favorites and nonfavorites. If autumn leaves change colors where you live, discuss the different colors.

Glue, tape, or staple perfect leaf specimens to five-by-eight-inch index cards. Ask the children to think of imaginary names for the different leaves, such as "pointy leaf" and "blobby leaf." Print the names on the cards. Match the leaves with pictures of leaves in leaf identification books to find out their real names. Print these names on the cards too, in a different color. Display the name cards on the bulletin board. Invite volunteers to read the names. Press other leaves, vein side down, on sponges soaked with paint. Lift and press on more index cards to make leaf-print cards. Match the leaf-print cards with the name cards.

Math

Playing Store

Together with the children think of how you could set up a play store in the classroom. Perhaps a desk set up as an adjunct to the housekeeping corner could be the store. Use a toy cash register and/or a plastic silverware tray for storing money. Make play money by tracing rectangular bill-size patterns on construction paper and cutting them out. Decorate the play money with numbers, pictures, and dollar signs. Number stamps and ink pads can be used to "print" money. Buttons, bottle caps, and counting chips can be used for coins. Egg cartons and muffin tins can be used for storing them. Removable pressure-sensitive labels can be used to mark prices on items. Encourage the children to take turns being buyers and sellers or "clerks." Put some purses and wallets in the dress-up box in the housekeeping corner.

Math

Money

CONCEPT: *Money is used to buy things. Money has pictures and numbers on it. The numbers tell how much the money is worth.*

Set a money display in the math center. Have different activities for the children to carry out there, such as:

1. Make coin rubbings. Put a coin under a piece of paper. Rub the side of a peeled crayon over the paper over the coin. A coin picture should appear. What is the name of the coin?

2. Draw portraits on paper money. Provide photocopies of a big, color-in dollar. Ask the children to pretend they grew up to be a famous president. Have them draw their pictures as president on the dollar. Have them draw numbers on the dollar to show how much it is worth.

3. Weigh money. Set up a pan balance in the money center and ask children to count how many pennies it takes to balance a small toy of their choice. Ask them to record their answers by drawing the toy and the correct number of pennies next to it. (Better still, have them draw a prediction ahead of time to compare with the results.)

Art

Designing and Printing Money and Stamps

CONCEPT: *Money is printed. We can make play money by printing it in class in a pretend "printing" factory.*

Dab coins lightly on sponges soaked with tempera paint. Press the coins, paint side down, on paper. Cut out the coins. If you want to use them for classroom play and hence to make them sturdier, cover them on both sides, after they dry but before you cut, with clear plastic adhesive paper.

Examine different kinds of paper money. Notice all the different kinds of pictures found on it. Collect classroom objects that can be used to print pictures on paper money. Some good ones are spools, cookie cutters, clothespins, autumn leaves, jar lids, number shapes, and alphabet blocks. Dab the objects on sponges soaked with paint. Press on index cards or other precut rectangular shapes.

VARIATION: Design and print pretend stamps for mailing letters in a classroom post office.

☆TIP☆

Place a section of newspaper under the paper you are printing on. The newspaper will catch spills and also provide a soft surface, which works better for printing than a hard one.

Art

Junk Sculptures

CONCEPT: *Instead of throwing things away, we can think of other ways to use them.*

Encourage the children and parents to contribute Styrofoam peanuts, shirt cardboards, toilet paper rolls, margarine tubs, string, bottle caps, boxes, catalogs, and other throwaways to a class "junk sculpture box." Keep a supply of junk materials in the art center, along with plenty of white glue, so that children can make constructions. Teach them to use box lids or shirt cardboards for a base and to clean up after themselves. Sometimes, ask the children to build imaginary constructions to go with themes you are studying, such as an imaginary vehicle that can go anywhere (for a transportation theme) or an imaginary place for animals to live (for an animal theme).

> INVITE SENIOR CITIZENS TO SUPERVISE REAL WOODWORKING PROJECTS IN YOUR CLASSROOM.

Music

The Mulberry Bush

Here we go 'round the mulberry bush,
The mulberry bush, the mulberry bush,
Here we go 'round the mulberry bush,
So early in the morning.

This is the way we wash our clothes,
Wash our clothes, wash our clothes,
This is the way we wash our clothes,
So early in the morning.

Help the children invent and act out new verses that describe what they do at home, in school, or in the community at large. For example:

This is the way we pick up our toys
This is the way we brush our teeth
This is the way we put away blocks
This is the way we walk in line
This is the way we cross the street
This is the way we wave good-bye

Recommended Records

□ *Holiday Songs for All Occasions* and *The Corner Grocery Store* by Raffi.

Music

Peter Hammers

(Pretend you're construction workers.)

CONCEPT: *Both men and women can be construction workers. Substitute different children's names for "Peter" each time you sing the concept. Make up other verses that tell what workers eat for breakfast, how they get to work, and so forth.*

(*Hammer one fist in the air*)

Peter hammers with one hammer,
One hammer, one hammer;
Peter hammers with one hammer
All day long.

(*Hammer two fists in the air*)

Peter hammers with two hammers,
Two hammers, two hammers;
Peter hammers with two hammers
All day long.

(*Hammer two fists and one foot*)

Verse 3: substitute "three hammers"

(*Hammer two fists and two feet*)

Verse 4: substitute "four hammers"

(*Hammer two fists, two feet, and shake head*)

Verse 5: substitute "five hammers"

(*Sing slowly and sway back and forth slowly*)

Peter's very tired now,
Tired now, tired now;
Peter's very tired now,
All day long.

(*Sing more slowly in a whisper and pretend to sleep*)

Peter's going to bed now,
Bed now, bed now;
Peter's going to bed now,
All day long.

(*Sing quickly, pretending to wake up*)

Peter's wide awake now,
Awake now, awake now;
Peter's wide awake now,
All day long.

Physical Education

Red Light, Green Light

CONCEPT: *Red light means stop; green light means go.*

In a gym or outside, establish a start and finish line. IT stands at the finish line. The other players spread out across the start line. IT yells, "Green light," turns away from the players, and counts out loud from one to ten, during which time the players run toward the finish line. When IT reaches ten, IT yells, "Red light," and turns back to the players. At the sound of the words *red light*, the players stop running and freeze. IT sends anyone still moving back to the start line. IT turns and yells "Green light," and the game continues. Eventually someone reaches the finish line and touches it. That person is the next IT.

VARIATION 1: Instead of yelling out the light colors, show green or red pictures.

VARIATION 2: Instead of yelling out the light colors, show signs with the words *green* or *red* printed on them, perhaps in green or red paint.

RED LIGHT!

Physical Education

London Bridge

London Bridge is falling down,
Falling down, falling down.
London Bridge is falling down,
My fair lady.

Build it up with iron bars, etc.
Iron bars will bend and break, etc.
Build it up with pins and needles, etc.
Pins and needles rust and bend, etc.*
Build it up with gravel and stone, etc.
Gravel and stone will wash away, etc.

To play, two children, one representing gold and one representing silver,† make a bridge with their hands. The other children march under the bridge in a line. On "My fair lady" the bridge makers drop their arms to capture the child underneath. The captured child has to choose gold or silver and then line up behind the bridge maker of that color. When all the children have been caught, the two lines have a tug of war.

Display pictures of bridges in the block center. Ask children to build bridges of blocks that look like the pictures.

My Fair Lady...

*In the science center place some iron objects and plastic objects in a shallow pan with water in the bottom. Leave for several days. Observe which objects rust. Do the experiment again with new objects the children choose to test. Have them predict whether the objects will rust or not and then compare their predictions with the experiment's outcomes.

†To signify the two bridge makers, make crowns for them out of cardboard covered with gold and silver foil. Or have them wear necklaces, one of imitation gold and the other of imitation silver.

Chapter 6

Theme: Food

A good month in which to explore this theme is November, the month of the final harvest and Thanksgiving. The goals of the unit are to help children learn about healthful foods and to provide them with firsthand experiences in food preparation. Such hands-on experiences foster skill development in all the curriculum areas: language arts, social studies, science, math, art, and music. Children like to cook, so this unit should be especially enjoyable for them. Cooking activities can continue all year, and healthful foods can be reviewed again when the topic of health is studied.

Language Arts: Oral Language

Poems to Memorize

Teach the children the poems so they can enjoy saying them together. Print out copies of the poems for each child to illustrate and take home. Encourage parents to enjoy and memorize poetry with their children.

Mix a Pancake

Mix a pancake
Stir a pancake
  Pop it in the pan;
Fry the pancake
Toss the pancake
  Catch it if you can.

     —Christina G. Rossetti

(Make pancakes in class, using an electric frying pan or stove. Keep children away from the heat.)

Little Jack Horner

Little Jack Horner sat in a corner,
Eating his Christmas pie;
He put in his thumb and pulled out a plum,
And said, "What a good boy am I."

(Make up new verses for real children and to fit the time of year.)

Little Gail Smith sat in a corner,
Eating her Thanksgiving pie;
She put in her thumb and pulled out a plum,
And said, "What a good girl am I."

To Market, to Market

To market, to market, to buy a fat pig;
Home again, home again, jiggety jig.
To market, to market, to buy a fat hog;
Home again, home again, jiggety jog.

(Make up other verses for other foods.)

To market, to market, to buy a fat pie;
Home again, home again, jiggety jie.
To market, to market, to buy a fat cake;
Home again, home again, jiggety jake.

Language Arts: Listening

Food Riddles

Ask each child to bring into class for homework some kind of healthful food, such as a carrot, a granola bar, a box of raisins, a can of peas, and so forth. Spread the foods out on a table to look at. Teach the children how to ask riddles about the foods, such as, "What is red on the outside, white inside, and tastes crunchy when you bite into it?" (an apple) Ask a few riddles yourself and then ask for volunteers to ask riddles. Explain to the children that they must listen carefully when a riddle is asked so that they hear all the clues.

VARIATION 1: Hide the foods in a box and ask each child to ask a riddle about the food he or she brought to class.

VARIATION 2: Collect magazine pictures of food and display them on a bulletin board. Ask riddles about them.

Recommended Read-Aloud Books

□ *Blueberries for Sal*, McCloskey (Viking)—A boy and his mother and a bear and his mother all go berry picking.

□ *Journey Cake Ho*, McCloskey (Viking)—how a hollering journey cake (pancake) saves a poor boy's family.

□ *Strega Nona*, DePaola (Prentice-Hall)—a wise old Italian woman has special powers and a magic pasta pot.

□ *Bread and Jam for Frances*, Hoban (Harper)—Frances refuses to eat anything more than bread and jam.

□ *Chicken Soup with Rice*, Sendak (Harper)—wonderful poem about the months of the year.

□ *The Carrot Seed*, Krauss (Harper)—a lovely way to learn where carrots come from.

What has a green top, is orange all over, and feels crunchy when you bite it?

What gives milk and goes "MOO"?

What are small, green and round and come in pods?

Language Arts: Writing

Two Class Cookbooks

Recipes We Invented

Ask each child to dictate a recipe to you. It can be for any food, perhaps the child's favorite food. Take down the dictation just as the child tells it. Don't correct the recipes. The results may be something like this: "To make spaghetti, throw the noodles in water and bake for 5 hours." That's okay. Ask the children to illustrate their recipes. Make photocopies of the results and collate into "cookbooks" the children can take home. These cookbooks make amusing presents for parents.

Recipes We Made

Make copies of the real recipes you make in class. Collate them into cookbooks the children can take home. Encourage parents to cook with their children. Put a safety page in the book with rules such as: (1) Children should not use sharp knives. They can use serrated plastic knives to cut and spread soft foods. (2) Children should not operate stoves or touch hot foods. (3) Children should only cook when they are with grown-ups. (4) Always wash your hands before cooking and always clean up afterward. Have each child decorate a cover for the cookbook.

Language Arts: Reading

Rebus Recipes

When you cook in class, write out the recipe in rebus form on language experience paper with the children watching. A rebus uses pictures to substitute for, or in addition to, words; thus, a rebus recipe is a picture recipe. Go over the recipe until the children can read it themselves. Encourage them to copy it if they like.

After the children are able to read the pictures on the recipe, provide them with ingredients and let them make the recipe. You may want them to work in small groups or individually if the measurements are given out in small enough quantities.

Social Studies

Food Factory

CONCEPTS FOR DISCUSSION: *We can share parts of a job. We can name the parts of a job in order (sequencing). A factory is a place where workers make things.*

Ants on a Log

1. Some children wash the celery.

2. Some children dry it.

3. Some children or the teacher cut the celery into logs. (Use plastic serrated knives.)

Social Studies

QUESTIONS FOR DISCUSSION: *What other snacks could we make this way? (Try Cracker Faces made by spreading crackers with cream cheese and designing faces on them with raisins.) What would happen if we put the ants on the log first and then the peanut butter?*

4. Some children spread the logs with peanut butter (or cream cheese).

5. Some children dot the logs with raisins (ants).

6. Everyone helps to clean up.

Science

Brainstorming Game: Same and Different

Set two different foods in front of the children and ask, "How are they the same?" Explain that there is no one right answer; encourage the children to think of many ways that the foods are the same. Repeat the process for the question, "How are they different?"

Interesting foods to compare are:

- Orange juice and milk
- An apple and an orange
- Grapes and raisins
- Flour and bread

Seeds Taste Test

CONCEPT: *Some seeds are nutritious to eat. "Nutritious" means healthful.*

At snacktime provide different kinds of edible seeds for the children to taste, such as roasted pumpkin seeds,* walnuts, peanuts, pistachio nuts, sunflower seeds, and popcorn. Explain that all of these foods, including nuts, are seeds. (You might want to explain further that not all seeds are for eating, and that children shouldn't eat seeds that come in seed packages. You might also want to say that food seeds should be chewed well before swallowing.) Make a chart with the seeds pasted on it and labels the children can read. Try planting some seeds. (see page 192.)

sunflower seeds
pumpkin seeds
peanuts

*To roast pumpkin seeds, mix 1 cup seeds (separated from the stringy pulp in a pumpkin) with 1 tablespoon oil. Roast for 45 minutes in an oiled pan at 200–250°. Salt, if desired.

Science

Sequencing: Before and After

To help children understand where foods come from, prepare different foods from scratch. Take photographs of the process to use later in sequencing games. Help the children use sequence words to describe when things happen, such as *before, after; first, next; then, finally; first, second, third, fourth,* and so on.

85

Math

Estimating Amounts

Ask the children to bring in food, such as dry cereal, that comes in countable pieces. Ask them to bring the food to class in clear plastic containers. Set the food on a table in the math center along with pencils, pieces of paper, and a collection basket. Ask the children to stop by the center at some point in the day to guess or "estimate" how many pieces they think are in the jar. Have them write their estimates down, sign them, and put them in the basket. When all the estimates are in, count the food pieces together into piles of ten. Then add the piles together to get the total amount. Ask, "Whose estimate was closest?" Help the children figure out the answer.

Math

Simple Simon

Simple Simon met a pie man
Going to the fair.
Said Simple Simon to the pie man,
"Let me taste your ware."
Said the man to Simple Simon,
"Show me first your penny."
Said Simple Simon to the pie man,
"Indeed, I have not any."

Ask the children to retell in their own words the story of Simple Simon. Elicit from them the fact that the story doesn't have an ending. Ask "What do you think will happen? Will the pie man give Simple Simon a taste even though he doesn't have any money?" Have the children draw pictures of their answer. For further discussion, ask "What could you do if you wanted something and didn't have any money to pay for it?"

Good vocabulary words to discuss in these discussions: *some, none.*

WHAT DOES "ZERO" MEAN ?

Little Tommy Tucker

Little Tommy Tucker sings for his supper.
What shall he sing for? White bread and butter.
How shall he cut it without any knife?
How shall he marry without any wife?

Elicit through discussion the idea that Tommy Tucker was a singer who was paid with free suppers for singing. Explain that doing something for another person can be a way of paying for something. Exchanging services is called barter. What else can people do when they don't have money? (They can trade things.) Help the children demonstrate the meaning of barter and trade.

I'LL SING A SONG FOR YOU IF YOU'LL READ ME A BOOK.

O.K.

Art

Peanut Butter Play Dough

Ingredients:

1 cup honey
2 cups instant nonfat dry milk
2 cups peanut butter

OPTIONAL: add chopped nuts, wheat germ,
or raisins to taste

Measure ingredients and mix them in a bowl, first with
a spoon and then with clean hands. Let each child get a
chance to mix the dough. Their hands will be oily. Ask
them to hold them up in the air until you give them a
paper towel and not wipe them on their clothing. Give
each child a ball of peanut butter play dough to play with
on a paper plate. When everyone is finished playing, they
may eat their play dough for a snack.

CONCEPT: *We can use our imaginations to make different
shapes.*

QUESTIONS FOR DISCUSSION: *What shapes can you
make with your ball of dough? (Try cookies, snakes, balls,
snowmen, peas, carrots, monsters.) How many different
kinds of shapes are being made? (Make a list on an experience chart.)*

Art

Food Dyes

Provide the children with scraps of natural color string, yarn, and muslin to dye in cranberry juice and blueberry juice from canned blueberries. Dry the string, yarn, and muslin and use to make collages. Explain that long ago people dyed cloth with dyes made from berries and other plants. Today many people continue to use natural dyes.

Pizza Pies

Make pizza pie collages on paper plates. Provide the children with construction paper, glue, and scissors. Ask them to think of foods that can go on pizzas, to cut out shapes to match them, and to glue the shapes on to the pizzas. Before the glue dries, let the children sprinkle the finished pies with yellow glitter for Parmesan cheese. If you like, you can also provide dried oregano to sprinkle on the pies so that they smell like pizza. Cut a pizza into four slices to teach the concept half and quarter.

Music

Popcorn Song

To the tune of "I'm a Little Teapot," sing:

I'm a little popcorn in a pot.
Heat me up and watch me pop.
When I get all fat and white, I'm done.
Popping corn is lots of fun. POP!

(The children should be crouched like kernels while they sing the song. On the word *POP*, they pop up in the air.)

Bring in a popcorn maker and make popcorn in class. Explain that the Wampanoag Indians taught the Pilgrims about corn. They taught them how to grow it and how to pop corn kernels. The Pilgrims had never heard of corn before. They were glad to learn about it.

Old MacDonald Food Song

Sing "Old MacDonald" a new way to emphasize foods that are grown on farms.

CONCEPT: *Animals and plants are grown on farms. Many foods come from animals and plants.*

Old MacDonald had a farm
Ee-I-ee-I-O,
And on his farm he had an apple tree,
Ee-I-ee-I-O,
With a pick-an-apple here,
And a pick-an-apple there,
Old MacDonald had a farm
Ee-I-ee-I-O.

Old MacDonald had a farm
Ee-I-ee-I-O,
And on his farm he had a pumpkin patch,
Ee-I-ee-I-O,
With a pick-a-pumpkin here,
And a pick-a-pumpkin there,
Old MacDonald had a farm
Ee-I-ee-I-O.

Ask the children to think of more verses.

Music

Food and Cooking Songbook

There are many food and cooking songs. Perhaps you and the children can make a class book of them with words and illustrations. The following list might be your table of contents:

"I'm a Little Teapot"

"Over the River and Through the Woods"

"Hot Cross Buns"

"Pease-Porridge Hot"

"Oats, Peas, Beans"

"Polly, Put the Kettle On"

"The Muffin Man"

"Sing a Song of Sixpence"

"Pat-a-cake"

Recommended Record

□ *The Corner Grocery Store* by Raffi.

Physical Education

Hot Potato

Ask the children to sit in a circle close together. Give one child a potato and ask him or her to start passing it when you start the music. (Play a tape recorder, record player, radio, or instrument.) When you stop the music, whoever has the potato holds it up, and everyone shouts, "Potato!" In this noncompetitive version of the game, it is good to have the potato. No one has to leave the game.

VARIATIONS: Play standing, tossing a big rubber ball to each other.

Physical Education

Peanut Hunt

Hide peanuts ahead of time on the lawn of the school or in a restricted area in a park. Before the hunt begins, define the borders of where the peanuts are hidden. Give each child a bag to hold the peanuts he or she finds. Give the signal for the hunt to begin. The children keep the peanuts they find. Have extra peanuts handy to drop near children who are having trouble finding them. Back in the classroom, have a bowl of peanuts handy for children who feel they haven't enough. If you like, make a graph of the amount of peanuts the children found.

Chapter 7

Theme: Sharing and Communication

A good month in which to explore this theme is December, a month of holiday celebrations. The goal of this unit is to help children learn to share and communicate in many different ways.

The importance of sharing and communicating is, of course, stressed all year long, but during December, when children may be overstimulated with holiday activities, a focus on sharing provides children with an opportunity to share their feelings and a focus on communication provides them with a broader way to look at the materialistic act of giving and receiving presents.

Language Arts: Oral Language

Storyteller Caps

CONCEPT: *A story is a way to share your ideas and feelings with others. A story can be a gift.*

Help the children make special storyteller hats from newspaper and tape. Decorate the hats with stickers. Ask the children to take turns putting on their storyteller hats and telling each other stories. Ask them to pretend that their hats are magic. When they put on their hats, their heads fill with stories to tell. Encourage the children to use interesting words, such as *happy, bored, angry, bashful,* to express feelings that the people in their stories might have. Encourage them to use these words to tell about their own feelings too.

VARIATIONS: When a child is running out of story ideas, he or she can give his or her cap to someone else to put on and finish the story.

Language Arts: Listening

Listening Game

To play, two children sit back to back so they can't see what each other is doing. Both children have similar sets of beads and laces. One child is the leader. The leader starts making a necklace, telling the other child the beads he or she is using. The other child listens carefully and copies the instructions. When the necklace is finished, the children turn to each other and compare. Are the necklaces the same? (They should be.) The children dump their necklaces and remake them, with the other child being the leader this time. Encourage the children to make patterned necklaces with their beads and to describe their patterns to each other.

Recommended Read-Aloud Books

☐ *The Rebus Treasury*, Marzollo (Dial)—Forty-one familiar nursery rhymes and songs are presented in rebus fashion for children to "read."

☐ *Do You Want to Be My Friend?* Carle (Harper)—A mouse searches for a friend among the other animals. You can tell which animal is next by its tail.

☐ *A Kiss for Little Bear*, Minarik (Harper)—a delightful story about loving.

☐ *The Giving Tree*, Silverstein (Harper)—A boy and tree grow old together.

☐ *Uproar on Hollercat Hill*, Marzollo (Dial)—A cat family fights and makes up.

☐ *Ask Mr. Bear*, Flack (Macmillan)—A make-believe bear tells a boy what he can give his mother for a present.

☐ *George and Martha*, Marshall (Houghton Mifflin)—Two hippopotamus friends work out their relationship.

☐ *Where the Wild Things Are*, Sendak (Harper)—A boy communicates with monsters in a journey of the imagination.

Language Arts: Writing

Writing Center

A rebus picture is a picture that stands for a word. In the writing center put a container of blank index cards and a container to hold finished rebus word cards. Make a rebus word card for each child with the child's photograph on it and the child's name on it. (The children can help make the cards.) Make other rebus word cards as the children want them. Encourage the children to send cards and messages to each other, using the rebus word cards if they want to spell something correctly. Tell them that they do not have to use the rebus word cards for every word; if they want to, they can spell words however they think best (invented spelling). As you study new units, introduce relevant rebus word cards to the writing center.

Message Center (or Post Office)

Set up a message center (or post office—call it what you like) where children can post messages to each other. The children can help make their own mailboxes as follows: Staple half a paper plate to a whole one to make a message holder. Decorate with a photograph of the child and the child's name.

Language Arts: Reading

Rebus Cards

Some rebus cards you might want to add to the writing center are:

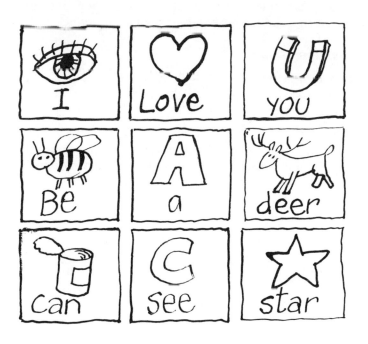

Rebus Picture Puzzles

To make a rebus puzzle picture, make rebus pictures without words and see if someone else can read your message. Try these messages: *I love you. Can you see a deer? Be a love. I can be a deer. You are a star.*

Social Studies

Learning Your Address

Write the children's names and addresses on big envelopes. Have them decorate their envelopes, and help them say their addresses aloud. Make a class mailbox by cutting a slit in a big cardboard box. (If you like, take the children on a walk to see what a mailbox looks like. Back in the classroom, ask them to decorate the cardboard mailbox to look like a real one.) Frequently, at circle time give the children their envelopes. Help them say their addresses aloud, and ask them to mail them in the mailbox.

Envelope Creativity

Ask the children, "What is an envelope?" Provide paper and paste, and ask them to create envelopes for cards they have made. Encourage different solutions to the envelope question. Make a bulletin board display of interesting envelopes.

Learning Your Telephone Number

Ask the children to draw or paint pictures of telephones. Afterward, write the children's phone numbers on their pictures. Let them copy the numbers if they like. Encourage them to memorize their phone numbers.

Telephone Game

At circle time hold a toy telephone in your lap and name a child. Ask the child to tell his or her phone number. Pretend to dial as the child speaks, and then have a make-believe telephone conversation with each other.

Put a few toy or nonworking real telephones in the housekeeping corner to help the children learn to say and dial their own phone numbers.

Social Studies

Authors and Illustrators

Explain that authors and illustrators are good at sharing and communicating their ideas. Authors write books, and illustrators make the pictures in books. Ask the children to select favorite books to share with the class. Show them where the author's and illustrator's names are written on the cover. If possible, invite an author or illustrator to visit your class to read one of his or her books. Have the children make books of their own to show the visitor.

Looking together at a real newspaper, talk about reporters, photographers, and newspapers. Have the children dictate stories about classroom pets, projects, and plans for a class newspaper. Type the stories, photocopy them, and collate. Or, if you have a computer, use publishing software programs, such as *Newsroom* (by Broderbund) or *Print Shop* (by Springboard), to help you make class newspapers and newsletters. These programs can make class dictation projects easier and more fun.

Leaders

Ask the children to tell you what a leader is. Elicit through discussion that a leader is someone others follow. A leader needs to be able to communicate his ideas so that others know what to follow.

Play Follow the Leader at circle time or in lines on the playground. If a leader's actions are unclear, stop and analyze how they could be better communicated.

The President of the United States is a leader. Post a picture of the President on the bulletin board. Look at other pictures of presidents in books, on paper money and coins. Make coin rubbings of presidents. (See page 69.) Talk about qualities that make a good leader.

Science

Light and Dark

Explain that in the summer the days are long because the sun shines a long time. In the winter the days are short because the sun shines for a shorter period of time. December is the darkest month of the year. For this reason, people like to celebrate with lights. Ask the children to tell how lights are used to celebrate December holidays. Some of the lights they may mention are Christmas tree lights and Hanukkah candles. Bring in Christmas lights to decorate the classroom and a menorah (Hanukkah candleholder). Ask parents to visit class and tell how lights are used in their holiday celebrations. Remind children to stay away from lit candles and matches.

Science

Hand Shadow Puppets

CONCEPT: *Hand shadows can be like puppets. We can use hand shadow puppets to share ideas.*

On a dark day turn off the lights and lower the shades to darken the room further. Shine a bright light (from a bright flashlight or projector) onto a white wall or piece of white cardboard. Let the children take turns making hand shadows on the wall. Encourage them to act out holiday stories with their shadows.

Science Questions

What makes a shadow? (A shadow is made by something blocking the light.) Why can't you find your shadow on a cloudy day? (The sun isn't shining; there's no light to block.) When is your shadow longest on a sunny day? (In the morning or late afternoon.) When is it shortest? (At noon.) Try measuring your shadows on the playground with chalk at different times on a sunny day.

DUCK

DOG

RABBIT

DEER

Math

Patterning and Paper Chains

Enliven the traditional holiday activity of making paper chains by asking the children to experiment with patterns in their chains. As the children work on their chains, ask them to tell what their patterns are going to be. Make a display by hanging all the patterned paper chains in one place and unpatterned paper chains in another. Explain that both kinds are pretty.

Measuring and Paper Chains

Ask each child to make a paper chain as long as he or she is tall. Have the children help each other hold their chains up to see if they are long enough or too long. Write names on the last link of each chain. Display the chains on the wall, each touching the floor to compare heights. Paper clip the chains together to see how long a chain all the lengths make when added together. Use the long chain to decorate the classroom. Just before vacation, take it apart so each child can take home his or her own section.

Math

Poem for Writing Numbers

A line straight down is lots of fun,
That's the way to make a 1.

Around the railroad track and down . . .
Tooot! Tooot!

Around the tree, around the tree,
That's the way to make a 3.

Down and across and down one more,
That's the way to make a 4.

Down and around; put a flag on top;
And see the 5 you've found.

A curve and a loop,
A 6 throws a hoop.

Across the sky and down from heaven,
That's the way to make a 7.

Make an S, but do not wait;
Climb back up to make an 8.

First a circle, then a line;
That's the way to make a 9.

Circle around to make a zero;
And you will be a great big hero!

Author Unknown

Help the children make counting books for presents. Explain that written numbers communicate amounts. Have the children make number pictures with written numbers and pictures of that many things. These pictures can be compiled into books for holiday presents for parents. The above poem can be retyped, photocopied, and inserted into the books so parents can say it with their children.

Art

Two Recipes for Ornaments

1. Mix and knead equal parts of white glue (pretinted with food coloring), flour, and cornstarch. Hand-form flat shapes. Embed large paper clips for hooks. Dry 2 days on waxed paper, turning several times.

2. Mix and knead 2 cups flour, ½ cup salt, and ¾ cup water. Roll out and cut with cookie cutters. Embed large paper clips for hooks. Bake at 350° F. for 10 to 15 minutes. Paint with acrylic or tempera paint. If you like, varnish the ornaments so they won't chip.

Holiday Pendants

Hang ornaments from long yarn loops to make simple necklaces the children can give their parents for presents.

Salt Beads

Make salt bead necklaces for presents from 4 cups flour, 2 cups water, and 1 cup salt. Mix, knead, and form dough into beads. Pierce with a straw and dry overnight on wax paper. Bake for 1 hour at 300° F. on an ungreased cookie sheet. Cool. Paint with tempera or acrylic paints. Dry thoroughly and string.

Wrapping Paper

Press cookie cutters lightly on sponges soaked with tempera paint, and stamp designs on tissue paper to make wrapping paper. Encourage children who want to make patterned designs to tell about their patterns.

Tags

Help the children write "to ——" and "from ——" on index cards and then stamp a cookie cutter shape on the card to make a gift tag. Show them how to punch a hole in the tag.

Art

Mexican Piñatas

CONCEPT: *People have different ways to celebrate holidays.*

To make a papier-mâché piñata, have the children dip precut newspaper strips two by six inches into flour and water mixed to the consistency of heavy cream. Lay the strips on inflated, round balloons. Leave room for a hole. Dry, paint, and decorate with strips of paper.

To make a paper-bag piñata, put several strong grocery bags inside one another. Fill with wrapped candy, small bags of peanuts, small boxes of raisins, and sticks of gum. Tie tightly and knot securely. Decorate with crayons, markers, and strips of paper pasted on the bag.

Suspend the piñata from a tree, ceiling, or broomstick held high in the air. Have the children take turns being blindfolded and trying to hit the piñata with a wooden spoon. When the piñata finally breaks, help the children divide the treats so that they can be shared equally. Teach the children ahead of time that equal means "the same number of."

(Imbed a paper clip for a hook into the papier-mâché.)

Music

Pattern Dance

Have the children stand in a big circle. Give them crepe paper streamers, alternating red, green, red, green, and so forth. Play music. Stand in the center, holding both a red and green streamer. (You are the conductor.) Wave your arms up and down to the beat, having the children move up and down to the music. When you raise your red streamer, the "reds" rise up; when you lower your green streamer, the "greens" crouch down.

Let the children take turns being conductor. Also, vary the patterns in the circle with different arrangements (such as red, red, green, red, red, green, and so forth) and different-colored streamers.

Music

Musical Instruments

Make tambourines. Decorate the backs of two sturdy paper plates with markers. Then put dry beans on one plate. Lay the other plate over it. Staple the plates together, making sure the decorated sides face out.

Make Mexican maracas (shakers) by filling plastic bottles with rice, paper clips, stones, or bells.

Make drums from coffee cans, pots, and salad bowls turned upside down.

Use the homemade instruments to accompany traditional classroom holiday songs.

Recommended Records and Tapes

- [ ] *Play Your Instruments and Make a Pretty Sound* by Ella Jenkins.
- [ ] *Learning Basic Skills Through Music, Vol. 5* by Hap Palmer.
- [ ] *African Songs & Rhythms for Children* by Dr. Carl Orff.
- [ ] *American Game and Activity Songs for Children* by Pete Seeger.
- [ ] *Rosenshontz Tickles You* by Gary Rosen and Bill Shontz.

Play Tchaikovsky's *The Nutcracker Suite* and let children draw or paint to the music, encouraging them to let their arms and hand move to the rhythms they hear and the emotions they feel.

Physical Education

May I, Please?

Play the traditional Giant Steps (May I) Game, emphasizing manners. To play, establish a start and finish line. The leader stands behind the finish line. The children spread out across the start line. The leader gives the first command, such as "Keith, you may take five baby steps." Keith then must ask, "May I, please?" If he doesn't say this, his turn is over. If he does, the leader can say, "Yes, you may," in which case Keith must say, "Thank you," and then take five baby steps toward the finish line. If he doesn't say "Thank you," his turn is over. To the question, "May I, please?" the leader can change her mind and say, "No, you may not. You may take three giant steps." Again, Keith must ask, "May I, please?" If the leader says, "Yes, you may," Keith must say, "Thank you," before taking the five giant steps. The first child to reach the finish line wins. As teacher, you can be the leader and manipulate the game that everyone wins once. Various steps are baby steps, giant steps, hops, jumps, twirl steps, backward steps, and leaps. Encourage the children to invent and name new ones.

Physical Education

Opposites Game

This game is a variation of the familiar game Duck, Duck, Goose. To play Duck, Duck, Goose the children sit in a circle. It walks around the outside of the circle tapping each child on the head lightly, saying "Duck" with each tap until It finally taps a player and says "Goose!" The Goose then jumps up and chases It around the outside of the circle, trying to tag him or her before It reaches the empty space. If It gets there first, the Goose becomes the next It. If Goose catches It, the same child is It again.

As you teach the children opposite words in the classroom, review them in this game. Instead of saying, "Duck, Duck, Goose," for example, have the children say, "Hot, Hot, Cold." Let the children think of opposites to substitute. Some good ones are *up/down, in/out, big/little, over/under, near/far, short/long, high/low, empty/full*, and *dark/light*. You and the children will be able to think of many more.

111

Chapter 8

Theme: Health

A good month in which to explore this theme is January, the start of the new calendar year and one of the coldest winter months. Often winter is a time when children suffer from common colds, sore throats, and earaches. Helping to understand how to stay healthy may help them improve their well-being. The goals of this unit are to help children understand the importance of good health and to help them learn how to promote their own good health.

Language Arts: Oral Language

Fingerplay

Five little monkeys (*place five fingertips on 'bed,' which is palm*)
Jumping on the bed, (*make five fingers jump*)
One fell off and bumped his head. (*rub head*)
Mama called the doctor (*hold phone to ear and dial*)
And the doctor said:
"That's what you get for jumping on the bed!" (*shake finger to scold*)

Four little monkeys, etc. (*make 4 fingers jump*)

Three little monkeys, etc. (*make 3 fingers jump*)

Two little monkeys, etc.

One little monkey jumping on the bed,
He fell off and bumped his head.
Mama called the doctor,
And the doctor said:
"No more little monkeys jumping on the bed!"

DISCUSSION QUESTIONS: *What are some different ways children get hurt? How can children prevent themselves from getting hurt? What safety rules do we have to help children stay healthy?*

ONE FELL OFF AND BUMPED HIS HEAD!

Language Arts: Listening

Listening to (and Giving) Instructions

Explain that when grown-ups tell children how to take care of themselves, they want children to listen to them. Have some props ready so that the children can take turns dressing up as grown-ups and telling the other children different ways to take care of themselves. The props might be a man's jacket and hat and a woman's shawl and hat. Encourage the children to think of different instructions grown-ups have given them for taking care of themselves, such as what to do when you fall down and get cut, how to brush your teeth, how to wash your hands, how to keep from spilling on yourself when you eat, how to cross streets, and what to do if you feel carsick. Perhaps to facilitate this talking-and-listening game, you might ask the listening children to pretend they are younger than they are—three-year-olds, perhaps.

Recommended Read-Aloud Books

□ *Bread and Jam for Frances,* Hoban (Harper)—a good book for talking about eating healthful foods.

□ *Bedtime for Frances,* Hoban (Harper)—a good book for talking about going to bed at night.

□ *The Three Little Kittens,* Marzollo (Scholastic)—the traditional poem about wearing, losing, and washing mittens in the winter.

□ *My Doctor,* Rockwell (Harper)—simple text and big, clear pictures.

□ *One Morning in Maine,* McCloskey (Viking)—A girl who lives near the ocean loses her first tooth.

□ *Doctor Desoto,* Steig (Farrar)—a humorous, make-believe story about a mouse dentist and a fox patient.

□ *I Read Signs* and *I Read Symbols,* Hoban (Greenwillow)—two clear and colorful photography books of road signs for children to read and study for safety reasons.

□ *Dinosaurs, Beware!* Brown and Krensky (Little, Brown)—Safety tips for children are taught by make-believe dinosaurs.

Language Arts: Writing

Washing Instructions

Ask the children to be "dolls' clothes washers." Have them dictate to you a process for washing the class doll clothes. Take their dictation down on the chalkboard, revising the process as the children revise it in their discussion. Elicit from the class the following steps: get materials, set up area for washing, wash, rinse, hang clothes to dry, and clean up washing area. When the class has agreed on a washing process that suits your classroom, divide the children into groups to do different steps of the process. Change groups from time to time. Take photos of the process or, later, have the groups draw pictures of the process. The children can write or dictate "washing instructions" to go with the pictures.

Looking at Dirt Through a Magnifying Glass

Provide magnifying glasses so that the children can look at dirt and grime on their hands, clothing, toys, and vegetables such as celery. Have them draw "before" pictures and write descriptions of what they see. Then, help them clean the dirt and grime away. Have them look again through magnifying glasses at the clean objects. Have them draw "after" pictures and new descriptions of what they see.

HINT: In cold areas, on a day when it is snowing lightly, take a magnifying glass outside and help the children look at snowflakes on their jackets. How many points does a snowflake have? (six) Back in class have the children draw "magnified" snowflakes with chalk on black paper, and write stories about them. Another art activity is to glue three popsicle sticks together to make a snowflake. Dribble paint on the sticks, and sprinkle with white glitter. Dry and suspend with string to decorate the classroom.

Language Arts: Reading

Reading Labels

Establish a bulletin board for collecting labels from cans and boxes. If you like, send home a note to parents requesting their help with the collection. Make a display of the labels, encouraging the children to read them and identify letters they know. Talk about the sounds the letters make. Save duplicate labels to make a matching game. Together, read the labels on classroom games and books. Draw pictures of new labels for familiar products or invented ones.

If you like, show the children the words *sugar* and *salt* listed in the ingredients list on food packages. Explain that eating too much sugar and salt is unhealthy. Have the children be "sugar and salt detectives" looking for foods that have these ingredients. Explain that if these ingredients are listed first in the list, they are the ingredients used most in the food.

Show the children the word and symbol for POISON on a container of poisonous material. (Perhaps the custodian could visit the class with some samples.) Teach the children never to eat or drink anything with that label.

Carrot Story

Have the children dictate and illustrate class stories about carrots and other healthful foods to eat. Display the stories and help the children reread them from time to time. Encourage visiting parents to play "secretary" with their children, taking down their children's dictation for rereading and display.

CARROTS ARE GOOD. YOU EAT CARROTS. YOU CAN MAKE CARROT SOUP. THIS CARROT IS BIG. CARROTS GROW OUT OF THE GROUND. CARROTS ARE GOOD TO EAT WITH PEANUT BUTTER. RABBITS LIKE CARROTS.

Social Studies

People Who Help Us Stay Healthy

Together, brainstorm a list of people who help other people stay healthy. List the people on an experience chart with a little illustration for each one. Ask the children to dictate a sentence or two explaining how each "health helper" helps people stay healthy.

If possible, invite some of these people to class to tell about their job. Ask them to bring special clothes they wear and some equipment they use to show the children. Have the children prepare ahead of time some questions to ask. They may need to practice asking the questions ahead of time in order to remember them and overcome shyness.

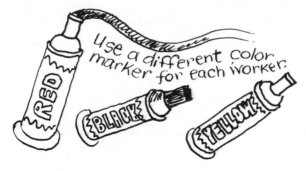

Use a different color marker for each worker.

Health Helpers

Dr. Harris

Mr. Watkin

Ms. Perry

Officer Fernandez

Mr. Smith

Social Studies

Solving Problems

Explain that people can be problem solvers and that solving problems wisely can help people be healthy. Spill a little water on the floor in the classroom. Ask the children, "How is this water a problem?" Elicit the answer that someone could slip on it. The children may think of other ways it is a problem—good; encourage many different answers, explaining that the more ideas we have for identifying and solving problems, the better problem solvers we are. Talk about ways to solve the problem of water on the floor in the classroom. Select a way that suits your classroom, and let a child do it, perhaps mopping up the water with paper towels. Ask the children to suggest problems to think about. If they can't act out problems for real in class, they can pretend.

Set out other problems for the children to identify and solve, such as: Why is broken glass a problem and what can we do about it? Why are matches a problem, and what can we do if we find them? Why is too much noise sometimes a problem, and what can we do about it? Why is too much activity and no rest a problem, and what can we do about it? Why is too much sitting and no activity a problem, and what can we do about it?

The Four Food Groups

Explain that there are four food groups: (1) meat, fish, poultry, eggs, and beans, (2) milk products, (3) breads and cereals, and (4) fruits and vegetables. Make a bulletin board display divided into four parts. Have the children contribute drawings and photographs of foods to sort into the four categories. Explain that a healthful meal has some foods from each group in it. Together, make and illustrate menus of favorite healthful meals. If possible, plan and make a healthful meal to serve in class. Talk about where the different foods come from and what kinds of workers bring them to us.

MEAT + FISH   MILK PRODUCTS   BREAD + CEREAL   FRUITS VEGETABLES

Science

How to Stay Warm

Fill three containers with warm water. Let the children feel the water to see that it is warm. Take the water's temperature and record it on a graph. Ask them, "How can we keep the water warm?" Encourage them to think of many different ways, such as putting a hat on a container and covering a container with a lid and a blanket. Together, select two ways to keep the water warm and enact these methods in the classroom. Leave the third container uncovered, asking the children which container of water will cool off first. An hour or two later, test the water again, recording temperatures again. Discuss questions, such as: Which water stayed warmest? Why? Which water cooled off the most? Why?

Discuss ways to keep one's body warm outside in cold weather. Have the children "show and tell" about jackets, hats, mittens, and so forth that they wore on the way to school to keep warm.

12:00			
11:00	76°	70°	82°
10:00	75°	75°	74°
	A	B	C

How to Cool Off

Explain that sometimes when we get too hot, we need to cool off. How can something hot be cooled? How can hot cocoa be cooled? If possible, make and serve hot cocoa in the classroom. Encourage the children to think of different ways to cool their cocoa so they can drink it, such as by waiting until the air cools it, by holding spoonfuls of cocoa up to the air until they cool and then drinking them, by blowing gently on the cocoa, by adding cold milk to the cocoa.

Ask the children, "When you get hot inside your snowsuit on a cold day, how can you cool off?" Encourage different kinds of answers, such as: by taking off your hat, by unzipping your jacket a little, and by stopping running for a while. Ask "Would it be a good idea to take your snowsuit off? Why not?"

Ask the children to dress up in the classroom in their winter overclothes and show how they cool off when they're outside. If you live in a sunny, hot area, ask children to "show and tell" how they cool off in the sun, such as by wearing a sun hat, by splashing water on themselves, and by making a fan from paper.

Science

How to Stay Dry

Do water absorption tests in the science center. Have children bring in items they want to test to see if they soak up water or not. Have the children make predictions, then test their items by dropping water on them. Record the results with pictures on charts. Ask the children to "show and tell" how they stay dry on a rainy or snowy day.

Math

How Many Bags of Flour Do You Weigh?

Weigh each child on a regular bathroom scale. Explain that the bathroom scale gives weight in pounds. Show the children how heavy one pound is by showing different kinds of food for snacks that weigh one pound, such as a one-pound box of raisins or a one-pound bag of apples. You will probably discover that kindergartners weigh about forty-four pounds, some more, some less.

On a sunny day have the children weigh themselves with bags of flour on the seesaw. To do this, you need to have a cardboard box, eight 5-pound bags of flour, three 2-pound bags or boxes of flour, and a few 1-pound bags or boxes of flour. (If you can't get flour, use another ingredient. Perhaps you can borrow the ingredients from your school cafeteria, and perhaps another teacher or the custodian can help you carry them outside to the slide.) Have the children take turns sitting on one end of the slide as you add bags of flour to the box at the other end. Have the children help you count how many each child weighs. Record the amounts on a graph. In the classroom weigh dolls and stuffed animals on a pan balance scale. Make individual pan balance scales (see page 69) for weighing lighter items.

Math

How Tall Are You?

Make a yarn graph to show how tall the children are. First, have the children draw portraits of their faces. Then measure them individually against the wall with yarn. Tape the yarn measurements to the wall, hanging the children's portraits above them so each child can find his measurement. Next to the graph, hang a tape measure. Help the children read the tape measure. (This is hard for kindergartners.) You will probably find that most kindergartners are about forty-four inches tall, some more, some less. Explain that eating good food and exercising help children grow the height they should be. It is natural for some children to be taller than others. Good vocabulary for this activity: *tall, taller, tallest; short, shorter, shortest.*

Art

Fancy Fruit Platters

CONCEPT: *We can serve healthy foods in beautiful ways.*

Provide cut-up fruit for the children to arrange in attractive ways on paper plates. After the children finish arranging the fancy fruit platters, they can discuss the designs and then eat them.

QUESTIONS FOR DISCUSSION: *How can we arrange fruit in patterns? How can we arrange fruits to make pictures? (Try making bunny salads with pear halves for faces, bananas for ears, raisins for eyes, and carrot sticks for whiskers.)*

MORE QUESTIONS FOR DISCUSSION: *What other healthy foods could we arrange on platters? (Try fresh cut-up vegetables, such as carrot sticks, celery sticks, cut-up green pepper, cauliflower, broccoli, and tomato slices.)*

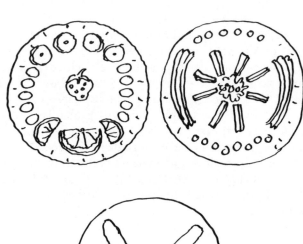

Art

Two Recipes for Soapy Finger Paints

1. Mix 1/2 cup laundry starch chips or powder, 1/2 cup mild soap powder, and 1/2 cup water.

2. Mix 1 cup water and 2 cups soap flakes. For both recipes, beat until thick with an egg beater. Divide into batches and add food coloring or tempera paint to make different colors. (These are good paints for getting children's hands clean.) Teach the children not to rub their eyes with hands covered with paint.

CONCEPT: *People can express their feelings through art. Expressing their feelings can make people feel good and healthy.*

To finger paint, have the children write their names in pencil on the slick side of dry finger painting paper. Then show them how to wet their paper with a damp sponge and how to finger paint on the wet surface. Encourage children to make finger paintings about different feelings, such as anger, happiness, and fear. Display the finished paintings, and talk about how they are alike and different. If you like, skip the paper, and finger paint on the table. Afterward, have the children clean the table.

Music

Lullabies and Marching Songs

Ask the children to think of different kinds of songs—songs for resting, going to sleep, counting, saying the alphabet, marching, starting the school day, and cleaning up. List the songs on an experience chart, each with a little picture to help the children read the titles afterward. Ask each child to pick a song and make an illustration for it. Write the title of the song on the illustration. When all the illustrations are done, ask the children to think of different ways to classify them. Make a book together of class favorite songs, putting various songs together in categories. Sing the songs, and discuss how the music in different categories is the same and how it is different. Ask "How are lullabies and marching songs the same? How are they different?" And "What is better for people, exercise or rest?" (Both are important.)

Safety Song

(Add this verse to the song "If You're Happy and You Know It, Clap Your Hands.")

If you're in trouble and you know it,
Tell a friend.
If you're in trouble and you know it,
Tell a friend.
If you're in trouble and you know it,
Then your face will surely show it,
If you're in trouble and you know it,
Tell a friend.

Music

Make a Tape for Rest Period

Make a tape of the children singing their favorite lullabies and quiet songs. If possible, accompany the songs
with music. If you can't play an instrument, perhaps another teacher, local musician, or parent can help you.

Let the children take turns borrowing the tape to bring
home so they can listen to it with their parents at bedtime. Ask the children to tell you when they go to bed at
night. If they don't know, ask them to find out for "homework" and to bring in on a slip of paper their bedtime
written down. Make a graph of bedtime hours. Explain
that people need sleep to stay healthy. The children
might want to memorize the following poem to recite on
their tape for rest period. Perhaps you can put it to music.
A related art activity would be to draw and compare
pictures of bedtime bedroom windows in summer and
winter.

Bed in Summer

In winter I get up at night
And dress by yellow candlelight,
In summer, quite the other way,
I have to go to bed by day.

I have to go to bed and see
The birds still hopping on the tree,
Or hear the grown-up people's feet
Still going past me in the street.

And does it not seem hard to you,
When all the sky is clear and blue,
And I should like so much to play,
To have to go to bed by day?

—*Robert Louis Stevenson*

Recommended Records and Cassettes

☐ *Learning Basic Skills Through Music—Health and
Safety* by Hap Palmer.

☐ *Movement with Music* by Cyril Ritchard. (Introduces
children to classical music through exercises.)

127

Physical Education

Exercises for Kindergarten

Can you fly like a bird?

Can you hop like a frog?

Can you stretch like a cat?

meow!

What other animal exercises can you do?

Physical Education

What's Inside?

Have the children rest and pay attention to their bodies for a minute at the end of an exercise routine. This is a good time to think about what's inside the body and identify internal body parts.

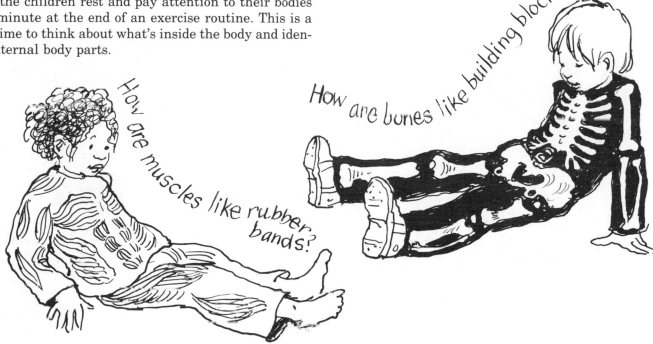

Chapter 9

Theme: Transportation

A good month in which to explore this theme is February, though it is a theme that lends itself to exploration at any time of the year. But in February teachers can use the theme of transportation to pull together a number of different kinds of February events, such as Presidents Day (discuss the kinds of transportation that Presidents Lincoln and Washington used long, long ago), Valentine's Day (discuss the kinds of transportation postal workers use), and snow (if it snows where you live, discuss the kinds of transportation used to remove snow from roads). Since February can be a month of inclement weather in many areas resulting in frequent cancellation of outdoor playtime, it lends itself to a theme that involves a lot of small and large motor activity. A special part of the unit on transportation can be a look at spaceships. The topic of space comes up again in chapter 11, Weather and Sky.

Language Arts: Oral Language

Poems for Recitation

Have the children draw pictures to go with these poems. Make photocopies of the poems for them to paste on their pictures. Encourage parents to memorize poems along with their children, explaining that memorizing and reciting poems helps children build oral language skills.

Engine, engine, Number Nine,
Running on Chicago Line,
If she's polished, how she'll shine,
Engine, engine, Number Nine.

Anonymous

A peanut sat on a railroad track,
His heart was all a-flutter;
The five-fifteen came rushing by—
Toot! Toot! Peanut butter.

Anonymous

Old Woman, Old Woman

There was an old woman tossed up in a basket,
Seventeen times as high as the moon.
Where she was going I couldn't but ask it,
For under her arm she carried a broom.
"Old woman, old woman, old woman," said I.
"Where are you going to up so high?"
"To sweep the cobwebs out of the sky,
And I'll be with you by and by."

Mother Goose

Language Arts: Listening

Word and Sentence Puppets

With markers, have the children draw faces on paper lunch bags to make puppets. On the bottom of each bag (now the top) print a simple word. Write the same words on an experience chart with pictures to illustrate them. Ask the children to put on their word puppets and call them by name. (Their names are their words.) Ask small groups of children to see if they can make sentences by standing together and putting their word puppets together. Help the children practice using the vocabulary words *first/next/then/last* to describe the position of letters in words and words in sentences.

Recommended Read-Aloud Books

☐ *Mr. Gumpy's Outing,* Burningham (Holt)—so many animals embark in Mr. Gumpy's boat that . . .

☐ *Freight Train and Harbor and Truck,* Crews (Greenwillow)—three imaginative books by the same author/illustrator.

☐ *Truck Song,* Siebert (Crowell)—Interesting rhyme tells about the journey of a transcontinental truck.

☐ *Trucks,* Rockwell (Dutton)—A variety of trucks are presented with a simple text and clear pictures.

☐ *Airport,* Barton (Crowell)—good information about planes and airports on a young child's level.

☐ *Stopping by Woods on a Snowy Evening,* Frost (Dial)—The famous poem of Robert Frost is interpreted with a story about a man traveling by horse-drawn sleigh through the woods.

☐ *Ox-cart Man,* Hall (Viking)—A long-ago farmer travels to the city and back with an ox-cart.

☐ *The Maggie B,* Haas (Atheneum)—A delightful little girl takes her brother on a make-believe journey at sea.

Language Arts: Writing

Five-Step Poems About Vehicles

Together write five-step poems on an experience chart. Each poem has five lines, and each line follows a format. As the children contribute lines, write their lines in different color markers to help them recognize and read back their lines later. The format for a five-step poem about a vehicle is:

TITLE: *Name of Vehicle*

LINE 1: size and shape of vehicle
LINE 2: color of vehicle
LINE 3: purpose of vehicle
LINE 4: where you'd like to be in the vehicle
LINE 5: name of worker who drives vehicle

Here are some examples of five-step poems about vehicles:

Race Car

Little.
Red and purple.
Goes fast and wins races.
On a race track.
Race car driver.

Back Hoe

Big with a scoop.
Yellow.
Moves dirt and rocks.
Construction site.
Back hoe operator.

Subway

Long like a train.
Silver and blue.
Carries people.
Tunnels.
Subway conductor.

Language Arts: Reading

Labels for Vehicles

Have the children bring you classroom vehicles to label. Use masking tape or pressure sensitive stickers for the labels. Ask the children to help you sound out the initial letters for each label, such as V for van. If you like, write the initial letters in different colors. If the children are able, help them sound out the rest of the letters in the labels. Encourage them to read the labels aloud as they play with the vehicles. Encourage them also to consult the labels on the vehicles if they want to write the words for the vehicles in their writing. Collect pictures of vehicles for a bulletin board display. Discuss the names written on them, helping the children to discover that they are often the names of the companies that own the vehicles.

Social Studies

Classifying Vehicles

Define three areas of the classroom as three special places: land, water, and sky. (The block corner might be the land, some tubs of water on a plastic cloth might be water, and an open space on the floor might be sky.) Divide the children into three groups: drivers of vehicles that go on land, drivers of vehicles that go in the water, and drivers of vehicles that fly in the sky. Ask them to find vehicles in the classroom that go in their areas and bring them to their areas. The children will discover that some vehicles can go in more than one area; for example, a plane can go in the sky and on land. Help the children decide for themselves what to do with a plane; they may decide to share it, or they may decide it goes mainly in the sky area, or they may come up with another solution. Encourage inventive solutions. Help the children decorate their areas to accommodate their vehicles. This can be a short half-hour project or a long project lasting days. Let the children visit each other's area with their vehicles, and encourage them to tell stories about their travels. Have them make imaginary vehicles that can go in all three areas. (See page 143.)

Social Studies

Wheelchairs

Have a student or guest who uses a wheelchair demonstrate how he or she gets about in the wheelchair. Explain that some wheelchairs are motorized and don't need to be pushed. Show the children how ramps are provided instead of stairs in buildings so that people in wheelchairs can get up them. Show the children how some stalls in bathrooms have extra wide doors to accommodate people in wheelchairs. If possible, show them how vans with hydraulic lifts can lift handicapped people into the van. Show the children pictures of the Special Olympics for handicapped people.

CONCEPT: *There are many ways handicapped people can get about.*

Science

Sink or Float?

Ask the children to find in the classroom things they predict will sink and things they predict will float. Explain that a "prediction" is a thoughtful guess. Help them record their predictions on an experience chart with words and/or drawings. Then test each item in a tub of water. Does it sink or float? Record the results on another chart.

Use a stopwatch to time how long it takes for things to sink to the bottom of a tub. Make a graph that records the amounts in seconds. Use the graph to compare which things take the longest and shortest times to sink.

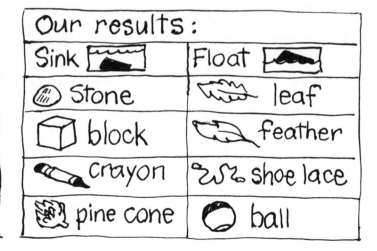

Science

Boats

Provide the children with a variety of materials with which to make boats, and ask them to create boats that float. Test the boats they make, and make a collection of the boats that actually float. Some boats to try are:

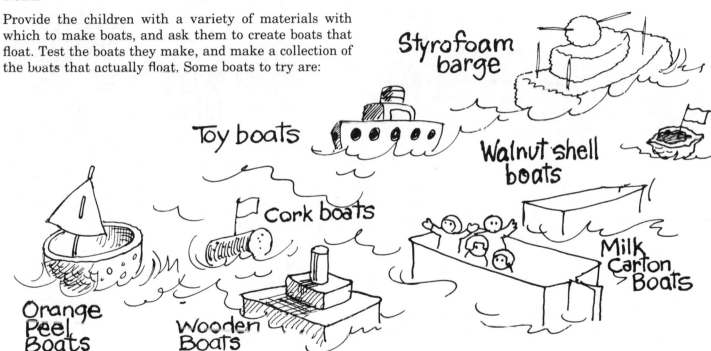

Styrofoam barge

Toy boats

Walnut shell boats

Cork boats

Orange Peel Boats

Wooden Boats

Milk Carton Boats

Math

Road Signs

Make a bulletin board display of pictures of road signs that contain numbers. If possible, take some photographs of road signs with numbers on a class walk around the neighborhood. Perhaps a parent could be the class photographer on the walk. Discuss the different signs in the classroom, helping the children read the numbers and learn what they are for. Have the children paint road signs with numbers to decorate the block corner.

Math

Transportation Graph

Ask the children how they got to school that day. Have the walkers, car riders, bus riders, bicycle riders, and so forth line up in different lines. Make a graph that has a column for each line. Illustrate the columns with little pictures (walker, car, bus, etc.). Give each child a sticker to paste in the right column. Discuss and compare the numbers of children in each category.

Ask the children to tell stories about coming to school. Help them review safety rules for walking and riding to school. Perhaps you can make safety murals emphasizing transportation. Invite a bus driver and crossing guard to visit the classroom and tell about their jobs.

TRANSPORTATION GRAPH

Art

Make a Class Train

Use the picture book *Freight Train* by Donald Crews (Greenwillow) or another book about trains for reference as you and the children plan to build a freight train in class. Talk about the materials you'll need, asking children to bring in from home adult-size and child-size shoeboxes and round oatmeal and cornmeal containers. Glue boxes to lids as necessary to form the cars you want. Punch holes in the boxes with a pencil (the teacher should do this), and connect them with pieces of shoelaces knotted with big knots. Lay the train on newspaper on the floor so the children can paint it. When it is dry, paint the names on the cars for the children to read. You might want to add a passenger car to your freight train, and follow that up with a class trip on a real train. A good

trip is to ride one stop, change trains, and ride back home again. Plan ahead of time with the railroad so that the engineer and conductors know you're coming. They may let the children visit the front of the train to see where the engineer drives the train. Back in class, let the children act out being train conductors. Make a page of cut-apart tickets with numbers on them. Photocopy the page, and have the children cut apart the tickets to make a ticket collection to play with. Give them paper punches to punch the tickets. This is a good activity for practicing number recognition as the children say, "Five dollars, please," and punch the number 5. Have the children tell and write stories about imaginary trips they could take on their class train.

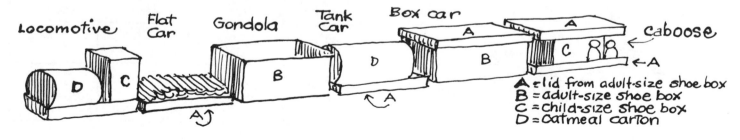

142

Art

Paper Airplanes and Helicopters

Show the children how to decorate paper with markers and then fold it to make paper airplanes and helicopters as follows. If they want to, encourage them to create new designs and see how they work. Measure how long airplanes glide by marking with chalk where they land. Time helicopters with a stopwatch to see how many seconds it takes them to fall. Record the times on a graph.

Imaginary Vehicles

Provide the children with an assortment of junk materials, such as Styrofoam, wood, fabric, toy wheels, feather, beads, paper, containers, paint, glitter, and glue. Ask them to invent imaginary vehicles that can go on land, water, and in the air. Have them build their vehicles inside box lids so that they can carry them home. Help the children label the vehicles with imaginary names. Have them tell and write stories about trips they took to Fairyland in their magic vehicles.

Music

Musical Balloons

This game is played like Musical Chairs. You will need as many balloons as there are children minus one. Have the children help you figure out how many that is (a good activity for practicing one-to-one correspondence). Perhaps you can have parents or older children visit the class to help you blow up the balloons. This game needs to be played outside on a windless day or inside in an area where there is sufficient space in which to move around. Play music (on a radio, record player, or tape recorder). As the music plays, the children bat the balloons around. If a balloon drops, that's okay. Just pick it up and continue to bat it around. When the music stops, each child catches and holds onto a balloon. Whoever is without a balloon becomes your helper. This person gets to pop a balloon with a pin so that there is one less balloon for the next round. Continue until the last child catches the last balloon and becomes the winner. An alternative and less competitive way to play (and one that saves balloons) is to *not* pop a balloon each time, but rather to identify the child left standing without a balloon with a good, friendly laugh, and then to continue the game, letting that child play again. No one ever leaves the game, and you play it for as long as you and the children like.

144

Music

Transportation Songs

Make a tape recording of the children singing transportation songs. Play the tape as the children are playing with class vehicles in the block corner. Let them take turns borrowing the tape to bring home and share with their families. If you like, make a transportation songbook to go along with the tape. The songbook can consist of photocopies of the words to the songs illustrated by the children. Some songs to include are:

"Down by the Station"
"The Bus Song"
"Row, Row, Row Your Boat"
"I've Been Working on the Railroad"
"She'll Be Comin' Round the Mountain"
"Yankee Doodle"

For a song about fire engines, sing to the tune of "Down by the Station":

Down by the fire station early in the morning,
See all the fire trucks standing in a row.
See all the fire fighters putting on their helmets,
(*Imitate a fire truck siren here*) Off they go!

Recommended Records and Tapes

☐ *Seasons for Singing* by Ella Jenkins.
☐ *Children's Greatest Hits, Volume II* by Tom Glazer.
☐ *The Aerobic Express for Kids* (Kimbo).
☐ *Water Music* (Handel). Play this as background music and ask the children to paint or draw pictures that have something to do with water.

Physical Education

OBSTACLE COURSE TRAIN

Together, make an obstacle course in the gym, or on the playground. Use old tires, tables, boxes, chairs, hoops and ropes to mark areas to go over, under and around. Have the children make a train by standing in a long line, and putting their arms on each other's shoulders. The first child is the "engineer" or leader and leads the others on the obstacle course. When the engineer's turn is over, he or she goes to the back of the line.

Physical Education

Jack Be Nimble

Have the children try different ways of jumping, for example, jumping with feet together, jumping on one foot, jumping without a running start, and jumping with a running start. Set up a starting line for jumps with tape on the floor or with rope on a playground. Measure how far the children jump with rope, tape, or chalk, whatever best suits your situation. Each time the children jump, you can chant:

Jack be nimble, Jack be quick,
Jack jump over the candlestick.
(The children can imagine the candlestick. Show them what one is ahead of time.)

When you chant the rhyme in class before a child jumps, substitute the child's name for Jack, for example:

Mary be nimble, Mary be quick,
Mary jump over the candlestick.

Chapter 10

Theme: Dinosaurs

Any month in the middle of the school year lends itself well to the exploration of dinosaurs as a topic. In this book we shall treat the topic as if it were being explored in March. Many teachers use the topic wind for a March theme, which is also fine. Such teachers should go ahead to the next chapter, which is about weather and covers both wind and the more usual April topic, rain. Some teachers find it interesting to study dinosaurs before or after the topic of spring holidays, such as Easter and Passover, because both holidays have eggs as a feature. Since dinosaurs were hatched from eggs, the topic of dinosaur eggs and Easter eggs can be related.

Language Arts: Oral Language

Real or Make-Believe?

Ask the children to bring to school dinosaur and/or monster models and toys. At Show 'N Tell have each child show his model. Ask "Is it real or make-believe?" Elicit through discussion the facts that:

1. dinosaurs are real, but there are no more left; we say they are "extinct,"
2. dinosaurs lived long, long ago,
3. dinosaurs lived on earth before people, and
4. monsters are make-believe.

Ask the children to divide the dinosaur and monster toys into two groups, real and make-believe. Have them work in small groups making dioramas for the toys. (Dioramas are scenes made of small objects in boxes.) Provide interesting materials for making the dioramas: art materials and various junk materials, such as yarn, ribbon, glitter, clay, twigs, stones, leaves, and sand. Ask the children who are making dioramas for dinosaurs to make the scenes real; ask the children who are making dioramas for monsters to make them make-believe. Encourage discussion as the children make their dioramas. When the children are finished, have them tell stories about their animals and scenes.

150

Language Arts: Listening

Spanish Words

Review the names of body parts, pretending you are dinosaurs and saying them aloud. Explain that different people around the world speak different languages and have different names for body parts. Say the Spanish names for body parts, asking the children to repeat them after you. Have the children share words they know in other languages. Make a tape of familiar English words and their equivalents in other languages.

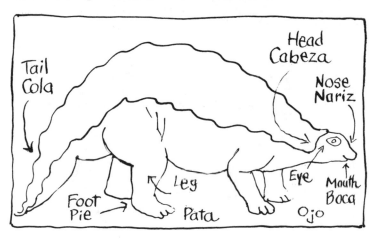

Recommended Read-Aloud Books

- *My Visit to the Dinosaurs,* Aliki (Crowell)—informational book for young children about dinosaurs and a dinosaur museum.

- *Dinosaurs Are Different,* Aliki (Crowell)—more information about dinosaurs and museums.

- *Dinosaurs, Beware!* Brown and Krensky (Little, Brown)—Home safety is taught by make-believe dinosaurs.

- *Dinosaur Days,* Milton (Random House)—a book about dinosaurs for beginning readers.

- *Flap Your Wings,* Eastman (Random House)—a funny picture book about a bird who hatches an alligator egg.

- *Prehistoric Animals,* Zallinger (Random House)—colorful, detailed pictures accompanied by a brief read-aloud text.

- *If You Are a Hunter of Fossils* and *Everybody Needs a Rock,* Baylor (Atheneum)—two picture books to introduce the topic of fossils and rocks.

Language Arts: Writing

Dinosaur Fact Books

As the children learn facts about dinosaurs, help them record the facts in dinosaur fact books. Explain that a "fact" is something true, and give examples of facts, such as: Johnny has red hair, and the school bus is yellow. To make the books, write, or have the children write, one fact per page. After discussion, decide what the dinosaur fact for the day is and write it on an experience chart. (Keep the facts simple.) If you like, put the chart in the writing center for the children to copy when it's their turn to be in the center. If the children use invented spelling on their pages, add a note to parents at the back of the book, explaining how invented spelling is children's natural, first attempt at writing and should not be corrected, but rather welcomed and enjoyed for what it is—a beginning attempt to express oneself through the written word. Have the children illustrate their pages and save them in folders. Do not hurry this project; perhaps the children can make one page per day. When they are finished studying dinosaurs, they can make covers for their books from construction paper and assemble the books. Bind the books either with staples or by punching holes in them and fastening them together with yarn or brass fasteners.

Some facts you might want to include in the dinosaur fact books are:

- Some dinosaurs ate meat.
- Some dinosaurs ate plants.
- Some dinosaurs ate both.
- *Tyrannosaurus rex* ate meat.
- He had sharp teeth.
- Brontosaurus ate plants.
- He had teeth like pegs.
- Dinosaurs lived long ago.
- They were reptiles.
- Snakes and turtles are reptiles too.
- Dinosaurs hatched from eggs.
- Some dinosaurs were big.
- Some dinosaurs were small.
- Some walked.
- Some flew.
- Some swam.
- There are no more dinosaurs.

Language Arts: Reading

Scientific Dinosaur Names

Dinosaur names are interesting to learn. Some of them have meanings the children might like to learn. Explain that *saurus* means "lizard." Show the children pictures of lizards, explaining that lizards live today, but that some scientists think dinosaurs were a type of lizard that lived long ago. (Other scientists think dinosaurs may have been a type of bird; nevertheless, the names of some dinosaurs have "lizard" in them.)

Tyrannosaurus rex ("tyrant lizard")—Explain that a tyrant is a mean boss who always has to be obeyed.

Stegosaurus ("plated lizard")—Make a big one on brown paper by taping green paper plates overlapping each other to form the dinosaur's plates.

Triceratops ("three-horned face")—Count the horns on his face.

Silly Dinosaur Names

Ask the children to invent silly dinosaur names, such as tree lizard (Tree-o-saurus) and pig lizard (Piggy-o-saurus). Have them draw pictures to illustrate their silly dinosaurs. Display the pictures on a bulletin board under the title "Our Silly Dinosaurs."

Social Studies

Long, Long Ago

Decorate the classroom with posters of dinosaurs, children's paintings of dinosaurs, dinosaur toys and models, and picture books about dinosaurs. Say to the children, "Let's pretend we could make a magic time machine that would take us back through time to the land of dinosaurs. The time machine will make us invisible so we could walk near dinosaurs and look at them and they would never see us. How shall we make this time machine? We need to make it big enough for all of us to fit inside." Have the children think of how to make it. Perhaps you can put the chairs in rows together like seats on a plane, or perhaps you can put blocks around the rug to make that the time machine. After you have made it, have the children "get in it." Pretend to work the controls and say a magic phrase, such as "Time machine, take us to the land of dinosaurs and make us invisible. 10-9-8-7-6-5-4-3-2-1-blast off!" Elicit imaginative discussion about flying through space and time, and about landing in dinosaur land. Have the "invisible" children get out of the time machine and look at the dinosaur pictures in the room, pretending that they are real. Have the children describe the dinosaurs—how they look, smell, feel, and sound.

Afterward, have them board the time machine again and fly back to modern day in the classroom to end the fantasy. Have the children write stories about their magic journey through time.

Social Studies

Paleontologists

Explain that paleontologists are dinosaur specialists. They dig in the ground to find dinosaur fossils the shape of dinosaur bones. (See pages 155 and 157 for more information on bones and fossils.) They bring the bones they find to museums and put them together to make dinosaur statues. Have the children pretend they are paleontologists digging for dinosaur bones. Hide in a sandbox the parts of a dinosaur skeleton model. If you don't have one, improvise dinosaur bones with Popsicle sticks, tongue depressors, and toothpicks. Have the children dig up the bones and put them carefully in a box or pickup truck to take to the "dinosaur museum." Have them record their findings with drawings and/or a dinosaur bones graph.

Museum Keepers

Make a dinosaur museum in the classroom. Have the children pretend they are museum workers and put together the bones that were dug up in the sandbox. If you have parts of a dinosaur model, have them put that together. If you have Popsicle sticks and toothpicks, have them paste those onto dark paper to make skeleton pictures. Count and record the bones in the skeletons.

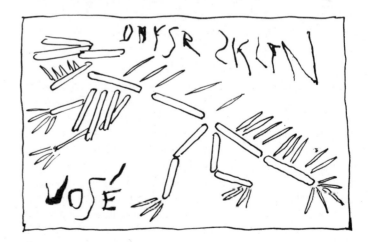

155

Science

What Happened to the Dinosaurs?

Explain that scientists don't really know why all the dinosaurs died long, long ago. They study the dinosaur bones/fossils they find and the earth where they find them for clues to the mystery of dinosaurs. The scientists have "theories" (unproven ideas) about why the dinosaurs died. Two theories are (1) a huge meteorite (rock) crashed into the earth, causing a huge explosion that put so much dust in the air that sunshine couldn't shine through it and the earth grew too cold for the dinosaurs and (2) the dinosaurs ran out of food to eat. Have the children make up theories of their own to explain why all the dinosaurs died. Take down their dictation.

When the dinosaurs died, they were buried with mud and volcanic lava. Lava is the melted rock that flows out of the volcanoes. Make a volcano in class, and have the "lava" flow over some dinosaur toys to show how they were buried. To make the volcano, fill a baking pan with wet sand, shaping the sand into a mountain around a large, empty clean orange juice can. Put ¼ cup baking soda into the can. In a measuring cup mix 1 cup water, ¾ cup vinegar, ½ cup dishwashing liquid, and 8 drops of red food coloring. Pour this mixture into the "volcano" and watch the "lava" flow!

WET SAND

HIDDEN JUICE CAN

PLASTIC DINOSAURS

156

Science

Fossils and Rocks

CONCEPTS TO DISCUSS: *Dinosaurs lived long, long ago—before there were any people. When the dinosaurs died, their bodies were buried in mud. Over time, the dinosaur bones turned into a special kind of stone called "fossils." People dug in the earth and found the fossils.*

Help the children make "fossil" handprints in class. Have each child fill a paper plate with wet sand. Then have the children press a handprint into the sand. Help the children fill the indentation with plaster of Paris made according to directions on the package. Let a little plaster of Paris run over the edge. Lay Popsicle sticks on the plaster of Paris for extra strength. When the "fossils" are dry, lift and brush the sand away. Display the handprints in a class "fossil Museum."

A prehistoric fossil collection containing a real fossil dinosaur bone and other real fossils is available from Insect Lore Products, Inc., P.O. Box 1535, Shafter, CA 93263. Write for a catalog or call (805) 746-6047.

1. Make a hand print in damp sand.

2. Fill with plaster of Paris.

PLASTER OF PARIS

Math

How Big?

Tell the children that the footprint of a *Tyrannosaurus rex* was three feet long and three feet wide at the widest part. Show them a yardstick, explaining that a yardstick is three feet long. Lay the yardstick on a big piece of butcher paper and mark off a space three feet long and three feet wide. Draw a footprint to cover the space. Cut it out and put it on the bulletin board. Have the children trace their footprints on construction paper and cut them out. Tape them to the dinosaur footprint, counting how many of their footprints fit in the dinosaur footprint.

Tell the children that Diplodocus was ninety feet long. Show the children a tape measure and use it to measure a length ninety feet long in the hallway or outside on the playground. Have the children lie down end to end to see how many of them are needed to form a line as long as Diplodocus.

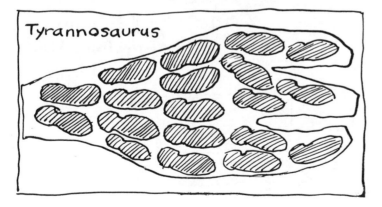

Math

How Little?

Tell the children that not all dinosaurs were big. Use a ruler, yardstick, or unit blocks to measure the size of a Procompsognathus dinosaur (3 feet or 1 yard long). Compare this size with the size of children and familiar classroom objects, asking: "What do we have in the room that is as big (or as small) as a Procompsognathus dinosaur?"

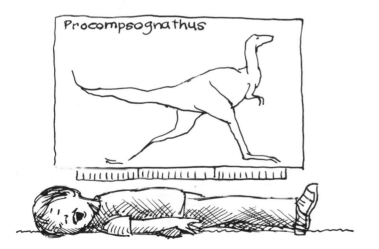

One-to-One Correspondence

Give the children toothpicks and Styrofoam peanuts (the kind used for packing material), and ask them to make small model dinosaur skeletons. Have them stand their skeletons in clay on cardboard. Display the skeletons in a class dinosaur museum. Count the bones in each skeleton. Help the children represent the skeletons more abstractly by drawing them with chalk on dark paper. Have them paste more Styrofoam peanuts on the drawings, using the skill of one-to-one correspondence to make the drawing match the skeleton model.

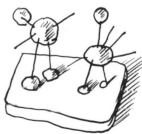

Art

Dinosaur Eggs

Explain to the children that Brontosaurus hatched from an egg about 10 inches long. Blow up a balloon that size, and ask the children to help you make it into a make-believe papier-mâché Brontosaurus egg. (You may want to blow up several balloons and make several eggs, or even one per child to take home.) To make the eggs, have the children dip one-by-six-inch strips of newspaper into a flour-and-water mixture the consistency of thick gravy. Show them how to run the strips of paper between their fingers to remove the excess water and then how to lay the strips on the balloon. Cover the balloon completely with several layers of newspaper strips. Dry completely and paint any color the children choose for a dinosaur egg. (Explain that since people didn't live when dinosaurs lived, no one knows what color their eggs were.) Make a nest in a box with clay, straw, yarn, string, paper scraps, and glue for the dinosaur egg, and write stories about the egg, perhaps about the egg hatching into a make-believe dinosaur that becomes the class pet.

Art

Rock Paperweights

Collect rocks to use for paperweights. Paint them to look like dinosaur faces.

Making a Stegosaurus

Stegosaurus had bony plates on his spine. Make a Stegosaurus in class by taping construction paper cones to the tops of boxes or bags. Cut eyeholes in the boxes or bags. Give each child a box or bag to put on. Have them hold onto each other to make the Stegosaurus. Hang a strip of paper with more cones off the last box to make a tail.

Polishing Rocks

Use an electric rock tumbler to enable children to change rough rocks into polished "gems." The polishing is done in various stages that are interesting for children to predict and later sequence with pictures or photographs. Classroom rock tumblers are available from Insect Lore Products, Inc., P.O. Box 1535, Shafter, CA 93263. Write for a catalog or call (805) 746-6047.

Music

Dinosaur Dance

Have the children pretend they are baby dinosaurs inside dinosaur eggs. Establish the make-believe eggs on the floor in a big area, one for each child, with hoops, chalk, yarn, or circles made with blocks. Ask the children to get in their "eggs" and curl up like baby dinosaurs. Then play "Night on Bald Mountain" by Moussorgsky or some other mood music suitable for dinosaurs. Ask the children to pretend they are hatching from their dinosaur eggs and learning to see the world and walk around in it. Ask them to move to the music. To end the musical fantasy, ask the children to pretend they are in a movie and that now you are running the music backward. Have them crawl back into their eggs and go to sleep.

Music

Dinosaur Songs

Adapt familiar songs to make them dinosaur songs. Perhaps the children will have some ideas for doing this. In the meantime, here are some you can suggest:

(To the tune of "One Little, Two Little, Three Little Indians")

One little, two little, three little dinosaurs,
Four little, five little, six little dinosaurs,
Seven little, eight little, nine little dinosaurs,
Ten little dinosaur eggs.

Name different dinosaurs you've studied and imitate them.

(To the tune of "Here We Go 'Round the Mulberry Bush")

This is the way I get around,
Get around, get around,
This is the way I get around,
Early in the morning.

This is the way I eat my food,
Eat my food, eat my food,
This is the way I eat my food,
Early in the morning.

Recommended Records and Tapes

☐ *Our Dinosaur Friends* is a record of dinosaur songs that can be dramatized. Words to the songs and suggestions for movement activities are provided. Write American Teaching Aids, Inc., P.O. Box 1652, Covina, CA 91722.

☐ *More Singable Songs* by Raffi.

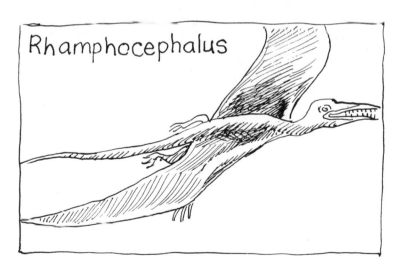

Rhamphocephalus

Physical Education

Dinosaur Games

Adapt familiar games so that they are dinosaur games. The children may have ideas for adapting other games; encourage their creativity.

Hot-O-Saurus. Play like Hot Potato but pass around a small dinosaur toy.

Pin the Head on the *Tyrannosaurus rex*. Play like Pin the Tail on the Donkey, but use a poster or child's painting of a *Tyrannosaurus*.

Dinosaur Swamp Toss. Toss small unbreakable plastic dinosaurs into a box.

Duck, Duck, Dinosaur. Play like Duck, Duck, Goose.

Physical Education

Stone (or Fossil)

Establish a start and finish line. All the players line up at the start line except one who is the Stone (or Fossil). The Stone crouches between the start and the finish lines. When you say "Go," the players at the start line tiptoe toward the finish line. At any point, you can call, "The Stone is alive! Run!" At this point, everyone runs to the finish line or back to the start line, and the Stone tries to tag players. If a player is tagged by the Stone before reaching either line, this player becomes a Stone too. Players who reach the finish line rest and watch the rest of the game. To play noncompetitively (appropriate for kindergarten), the last player to be made a Stone becomes the next one to yell "The Stone is alive! Run!" in the next round.

Chapter 11

Theme: Weather and Sky

A good month in which to explore this theme is April, a rainy, "weather-filled" month in many areas. Other good months are March (which, according to the saying, comes in like a lion and goes out like a lamb), February (good for studying winter and, especially on February 2, Groundhog Day, the concept of forecasting how long it will be until spring), and January (good for studying snow and ice). The theme of weather can be related to an ongoing look at the four seasons, starting in the fall with autumn. It can also be related, as it is in this chapter, with a focus on the sky and space. Space, itself an exciting topic for kindergartners, can become a month-long theme. However you approach the topic of weather, the four seasons, the sky, and space, you'll find that many of the activities can be repeated throughout the year.

Language Arts: Oral Language

Poems for Reciting and Memorization

April

Two little clouds one April day
  Went sailing across the sky.
They went so fast that they bumped their heads,
  And both began to cry.

The big round sun came out and said,
  "Oh, never mind, my dears,
I'll send all my sunbeams down
  To dry your fallen tears."

  Author Unknown

Clouds

White sheep, white sheep,
On a blue hill
When the wind stops
You all stand still.
When the wind blows
You walk away slow.
White sheep, white sheep,
Where do you go?

  —*Christina G. Rossetti*

It's Raining, It's Pouring

It's raining, it's pouring,
The old man is snoring,
He went to bed
And bumped his head
And couldn't get up in the morning.

  Mother Goose

Weather

Whether the weather be fine
Or whether the weather be not,
Whether the weather be cold
Or whether the weather be hot,
We'll weather the weather
Whatever the weather,
Whether we like it or not.

  Author Unknown

Rain

The rain is raining all around,
It falls on field and tree,
It rains on the umbrellas here
And on the ships at sea.

  —*Robert Louis Stevenson*

Language Arts: Listening

Father Wind and Mother Wind Poems

Draw two cloud faces (Father Wind and Mother Wind) on an experience chart and have them tell about themselves, as in "I am . . ." This activity helps children listen for and identify telling words (adjectives). If you like, repeat the activity on other days for Father Sun, Mother Moon, a drop of water, a rainbow, a pair of boots, and an umbrella.

Who has seen the wind?
Neither I nor you:
But when the leaves hang trembling,
The wind is passing through.

Who has seen the wind?
Neither you nor I:
But when the trees bow down their heads,
The wind is passing by.

—*Christina G. Rossetti*

Recommended Read-Aloud Books

☐ *Umbrella*, Yashima (Viking)—A girl waits for a rainy day so she can wear her new boots and carry her new umbrella.

☐ *Bringing the Rain to Kapiti Plain: A Nandi Tale*, Aardema (Dial)—A clever boy devises a plan to save the plains from a drought.

☐ *Gilberto and the Wind*, Ets (Viking)—A Mexican boy discovers the wind as a playmate.

☐ *Sailing with the Wind*, Locker (Dial)—A girl and her uncle sail a boat down the river to the ocean.

☐ *Dreams*, Spier (Doubleday)—Children invent stories to go with the changing shapes of clouds.

☐ *Happy Birthday, Moon*, Asch (Prentice-Hall)—A child plucks a star from the sky and brings it home for a short visit.

☐ *Goodnight, Moon*, Brown (Harper)—the best goodnight book ever.

☐ *A Day in Space*, Lord and Epstein (Scholastic)—Interesting photos show a day in the life of an astronaut.

☐ *Know the Stars*, Rey (Scholastic)—good background information for the teacher about constellations.

Language Arts: Writing

Star Light, Star Bright

Star light, star bright,
First star I've seen tonight,
I wish I may, I wish I might
Get the wish I wish tonight.

Make language experience paper for the children with a space on top for drawing. Read the children the poem above, and ask them to draw and write about their wishes.

If I Were . . .

Ask the children to pretend they are Mother or Father Wind, and ask them to draw and write what they see as they blow over the world. Afterward, have the children read their stories aloud to each other. Explain to parents that you accept invented spelling as a way of encouraging children to want to learn to write, much as parents accept baby talk as a way of encouraging babies to want to learn to speak.

Language Arts: Reading

Names of Stars and Constellations

Show the children pictures of constellations in star books, such as *Know the Stars* by H. A. Rey (Scholastic). Teach the children the names of some constellations, explaining that they got their names long ago from people who told stories about them. Help the children count stars in constellations. Give them blue or black construction paper, chalk, and big star stickers. Ask them to make constellation pictures, real or make-believe. Explain that they should put their stickers between their drawn lines, not on top of them, because stickers probably won't stick to chalk. Help the children write the names of their constellations on their pictures. Afterward, have them tell stories about their constellations. To extend this activity in the area of math, you and the children can make a bar graph to record how many stars each child put in his or her constellation. Use stickers to record the stars.

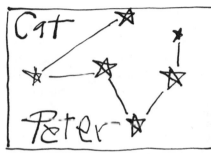

171

Social Studies

Weather Forecasters

Explain that weather forecasters keep track of the weather and make predictions about the weather for days coming. If possible, make a brief videotape of a TV weather forecaster and show it to the children in class. Ask them to pretend they are weather forecasters, using three tools to measure the weather: a thermometer, a rain gauge, and a wind indicator.

Thermometer

Mount, or have the custodian mount, a big outdoor thermometer outside a classroom window, out of the sun. If your window gets too much sun, find another place to mount it, such as a tree or classroom across the hall. Help the children read the thermometer, and record the readings for a week on a daily basis. Each day, ask the children to predict what they think the next day's reading will be. Record the prediction.

Rain Gauge

With the children, put a ruler or a stack of Legos in a coffee can, and set the can outside where it won't tip over and where it will be easy to observe. Help the children measure the water in the can after a rainfall. ("It's now two big lines high" or "It's now three legos high.") Record rainfall for a month and graph the results on a bar graph. At the end of the month, ask the children, "Did we have a rainy month, a dry month, or an in-between month?" Ask them to predict rainfall for the coming month.

Wind Indicator

Make a wind indicator with the children by hanging a piece of yarn to a tree branch or climbing apparatus. If possible, hang it where you can see it from inside the classroom.

Social Studies

Astronauts and Astronomers

Ask the children to make a big make-believe spaceship in the classroom so you can take a pretend voyage to the moon. Solicit the children's ideas for making the spaceship and outfitting it for the voyage. You might want to outline it with tape or blocks on the floor and put chairs inside for everyone, or just pretend the rug where you gather for discussion is now a spaceship. For the voyage make aluminum badges and/or hats to wear. Glue nuts and bolts to paper plates to make control panels for each child to "work" during blast-off. Ask the children to bring in cardboard paper towel tubes to use as telescopes. En route to the moon, ask the children to look out of their telescopes and describe what they see. (They might like to pretend they are seeing "for real" classroom posters of space objects.) Serve juice in space in plastic bags tied with twist ties around straws, explaining that in space there is no gravity—juice won't stay down in a cup. When you reach the moon, have the children get out of ("disembark from") the spaceship. Show them how to walk in a place without gravity (in a bouncy, slow-motion sort of way). Have them plant a class flag (made ahead of time) on the moon. (To do this, tack it to a picture of the moon

on the bulletin board.) Have the children get back in the spaceship ("embark") and blast off for the journey home. After they've landed, have them tell (perhaps on tape) and write about their voyage in space.

STRAW

TWIST TIE

PLASTIC BAG

JUICE

ASTRONAUTS HAVE TO DRINK OUT OF SEALED CONTAINERS LIKE THIS ONE, SO THAT THE JUICE WON'T FLY OUT ALL OVER THE PLACE.

Science

Wind Experiments

1. Dip a Ping-Pong ball in paint and set it near the edge of a table covered with brown butcher paper. Have a child blow the Ping-Pong ball as far as he or she can. The paint will leave a trail. Mark the trail with the child's name. Dip the ball in clean water, dry it, and dip it again in paint, perhaps another color. Have another child blow it across the same sheet of paper. Give every child a chance to make a trail. Concepts to elicit: *The harder you blow, the farther you push the ball.*

2. Have the children try moving different objects with wind power, that is, by blowing at them. Have them predict which objects will be harder to move and then test their predictions. Concepts to elicit: *Light objects are easier to move than heavy objects. You can move light, flat objects (like paper) if you get wind under them. Heavy objects with wheels are easier to move than objects without wheels.*

3. To practice blowing through straws, let the children blow through a little juice in the bottom of their cups at snacktime to make bubbles. Once the children are adept at blowing through straws, have them see what will happen if they blow through straws at paint. Spoon a little thinned tempera paint onto paper. Advise the children to blow at the paint from the side, not from the top. Concept to elicit: *Wind power can move thin, wet paint.* Display the straw-blowing pictures and have the children discuss their shapes, telling stories about any that look like real things.

4. Have the children make flags by drawing with markers or painting flag designs on rectangles of cloth. Tape the cloth to the table with masking tape to hold it steady while the children color. Have the children take their finished flags outside at recess. Have them predict what will happen when they hold them up in the air, and then have them test their predictions. Concept to elicit: *On windy days flags flutter in the air; on windless days flags droop.*

Science

Water Experiments

1. At the beginning of class, have the children predict how many different ways they will use water at school that day. Write their predictions on an experience chart, illustrating each prediction with a little picture to help the children read the chart. Check off the predictions as they come true and add to the list ways not anticipated.

2. Put one glass of water on the counter in the sun and one in the shade. Put a thermometer in each, and help the children identify and record the two water temperatures. At various intervals, predict changes in the water temperatures and test the waters with the thermometer, comparing the differences. Concept to elicit: *The sun has the power to warm things; we call this power "solar power." Shade blocks the sun and keeps things cool.*

3. Provide a funnel and plastic tubing for children to experiment with at the water table. Give them problems to solve, such as: How can you make water run slowly down a plastic tube? How can you make it run quickly through a tube? How can you stop it from flowing altogether? Encourage the children to predict results and test predictions.

Math

Classroom Calendar

To make a classroom calendar, cover a bulletin board (perhaps a freestanding one that you can wheel to the rug area for discussion) with construction paper. Mark off a calendar grid with yarn. Pin signs for the name of the month and days of the week across the top. Make two-inch-square oaktag number cards with the numbers 1 to 9 on them. Make fifteen 1s and 2s, five 3s, four of the numbers 4 to 9, and four 0s. Put these "date numbers" in a big fishbowl on a table near the calendar. In another fishbowl, put cut-out "weather pictures" that symbolize weather—a sun for sunny weather, a cloud for cloudy weather, a raindrop for rainy weather, and a snowflake for snowy weather. In still another fishbowl, put cut-out "special day" pictures—cakes for birthdays and stars for special occasions, such as trips, parties, holidays, and plays. Each day, ask the children to help you record news about the day on the calendar, identifying the date and selecting numbers and pictures to mark the date, identifying the weather and selecting pictures to mark the day's weather, and identifying the day's special events and selecting (or perhaps making) pictures to mark the events. Write on the cakes the names of the children having birthdays and on the stars names of special events.

At the end of each month, review the month's weather and events before taking down the numbers and pictures to get ready for the new month.

Math

Measuring Puddles

Go outside after it rains and find a puddle on the playground. Give the children chalk and let them trace the puddle's outline. Ask the children to predict what will happen to the puddle in an hour's time. Record the predictions on an experience chart, go inside for an hour, and then go back outside to see if the predictions have come true. Trace again the puddle's outline with another color chalk. Repeat activity at later activities, if possible. When the puddle is dry, lay different color yarns on the different color chalk lines. Cut the yarn to fit and bring the pieces into the classroom. Compare their lengths and use them to make a puddle on the floor or bulletin board. Give the children colored chalk to make puddle pictures on dark paper. Have them tell and write stories about puddles. Concept to elicit: *Puddles shrink and dry ("evaporate") in the sun.*

Measuring Shadows

Go outside in the morning on a bright, sunny day, and have the children trace each other's shadows on the playground with chalk. Ask the children to predict what will happen to their shadows in an hour's time. Record the predictions on an experience chart, go inside for an hour, and then go back outside to see if the predictions have come true. Trace again the shadows' outlines with another color chalk. Repeat activity at later activities, if possible. What happens? Concepts to elicit: *When the sun shines on you from the side, you have a shadow. The sun rises in the sky during the day. As the sun rises, your shadow shrinks. At noon, the sun is over head and your shadow is the smallest.*

On a dark day, make shadow ("silhouette") pictures inside by tracing the children's profiles on dark paper. Create the profile by shining a projector light on them. Have the children cut out their profiles and display. Ask "Can you recognize your profiles?" More shadow activities: make shadow puppets and play Shadow Tag.

Art

Bubbles

Make giant bubbles outside on a sunny day and watch them float in the air. Ask the children, "What colors do you see in the bubbles? What pictures do you see in the bubbles?" (Concept: *Bubbles act like lenses and show upside-down pictures.*) To make the bubble solution, in a baking pan mix 8 tablespoons liquid dishwashing soap (such as Joy or Ajax) with 1 quart water. (To make better bubbles, add a tablespoon of glycerine, available in pharmacies.) Ahead of time, use a can opener to remove both ends of round tin cans. Make sure there are no sharp metal edges. (You might ask in a parent newsletter for parents to send prepared cans to school with the children. Other things that can be used to make bubbles are six-pack holders, berry baskets, colanders, and pipe cleaners bent in a circle.) To make the bubbles, dip a can into the soap solution. Slowly pull the can out so that a film of soap remains on one end. Gently pull the can through the air or blow into it to make a bubble appear. Twist the can to release the bubble. Explain to the children that making giant bubbles takes practice. Who will be the first to do it? Make small bubbles from commercial bubble holders or holders made from pipe cleaners. Later, draw bubble pictures on paper plates and display them upside-down on the bulletin board. A good book about blowing bubbles is *Bubbles: A Children's Museum Activity Book* by Bernie Zubrowski (Little, Brown).

Art

Kites

Give each child a lunch bag to decorate with markers. Fold the open edge of the bag back about one and a half inches. Tape a five-inch piece of kite string to each corner of the bag with strong tape. Join the four strings together with a knot. Attach a long piece of string (about five to six feet) to the knot. To fly the kite, hold the string, let the bag go behind you, and run. Do this on a windy day in an open area away from trees and electrical wires. Concept: *Wind power holds kites up in the air.*

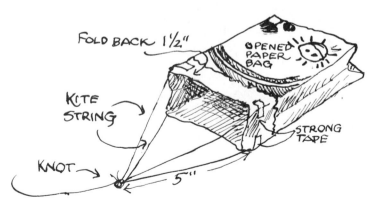

Rainbows

To make a rainbow, stand outside and spray a fine mist from a hose into the air. Ahead of time, ask the children to predict where you should stand to make the best rainbow—with the sun behind you, next to you, or in front of you? Have the children record the results of the experiment with drawings or paintings of rainbows. Ask them "What colors are found in rainbows?" Have them look at photos of rainbows to discover that real rainbows always have their colors in the same order, which is, starting from the inside, purple, blue, green, yellow, orange, and red. (These are the same colors that are seen in bubbles and when light passes through a prism.) Make rainbows in class with paint, colored clay, or by pasting yarn on blue paper. Do not insist that the children make their rainbow colors authentic.

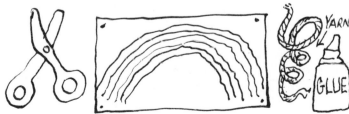

Music

Dramatic Improvisation

Help the children improvise movements to go with this poem. Read the poem aloud a few times, and then, reading it line by line, ask them to act out the story. Encourage the children to make up the fantasy together. They may all want to be flowers, or some can be flowers while others dramatize other parts. Together, select music to play as a background to the poem, or use musical instruments to express different parts of the poem.

Nature's Wash Day

Mother Nature had a wash day
  And called upon the showers
To bathe the dusty faces
  Of the little roadside flowers.
She scrubbed the green grass carpet
  Until it shone like new.
She washed the faded dresses
  Of the oaks and maples too.
No shady nook or corner
  Escaped her searching eye,
And then she sent the friendly sun
  To shine and make them dry.

    Author Unknown

Music

Rainbow Garden Song

Make a rainbow garden on a bulletin board by cutting out and pasting seed catalog pictures of flowers in rainbow stripes on a big sheet of paper. Afterward, sing to the tune of "Sing a Song of Sixpence":

Sing a song of rainbows,
In our kindergarten,
We have many colors
Growing in our garden,
Flowers come in all colors
To cheer up you and me,
We put them in a rainbow
For everyone to see.

Recommended Records and Tapes

☐ *I Know the Colors in the Rainbow* by Ella Jenkins with children from St. Vincent de Paul Center of Chicago.

☐ *It's the Truth* by Rosenshontz.

Wind Song

Outside, on a windy day, find things that are blowing in the wind and sing verses about them to the tune of "The Farmer in the Dell."

The wind blows the flag,
The wind blows the flag,
On a very windy day,
The wind blows the flag.

Physical Education

Shadow Tag

Early or late on a sunny day when shadows are long, play shadow tag. Play like regular tag, only to catch someone you have to step on their shadow.

Squirt Gun Bull's-Eye

On a warm, sunny day let children shoot bull's-eyes with squirt guns. Draw the bull's-eyes with chalk on the ground. Try shooting bubbles too.

Physical Education

Swinging

Ask the children to tell what they like to do on swings.
Read them this poem and put it on a tape for the children
to listen to in the listening center. Encourage the children
to memorize it and say it to themselves when they are
swinging. Review safety rules pertaining to swings, such
as *Don't jump off* and *Never run in front or behind the
swings because you might get hit.*

How do you like to go up in a swing,
  Up in the air so blue?
Oh, I do think it the pleasantest thing
  Ever a child can do!

Up in the air and over the wall,
  Till I can see so wide,
Rivers and trees and cattle and all
  Over the countryside—

Till I look down on the garden green,
  Down on the roof so brown—
Up in the air I go flying again,
  Up in the air and down!

  —*Robert Louis Stevenson*

Chapter 12

Theme: Plants

A good month in which to explore this theme is May or an earlier spring month. May is especially suitable because children can give plants to their mothers for Mother's Day. The theme of plants can be anticipated a month earlier if you start plants from seed six to eight weeks ahead of time. (See page 192.) Other alternatives for Mother's Day presents are to transplant plants purchased in flats into individual containers for gifts (see page 192) and to make paper flower bouquets (see page 196). The theme of plants can also be anticipated in the fall with activities such as leaf gathering, seed collecting, and bulb planting. Many of the fall activities regarding leaves, seeds, and flowers can be recorded, saved, and compared with related activities in the spring.

Language Arts: Oral Language

Sentence Patterns

Help children hear and reproduce sentence patterns by changing the words in the following nursery rhyme:

Mary, Mary, quite contrary,
How does your garden grow?
With silver bells and cockleshells,
And pretty maids all in a row.

Explain that "silver bells," "cockleshells," and "pretty maids" are names for flowers that look like bells, shells, and girls dressed up in party clothes. Ask the children to imagine flowers that look like these and other familiar things, such as spoons, balls, or stars. Have them color pictures of make-believe gardens with the flowers they have imagined. (If you like, provide patterns to trace and cut out of construction paper.) Discuss the pictures together, inviting children to tell about their gardens using the Mary, Mary question-and-answer format as follows:

(You say)

Michael, Michael, quite contrary,
How does your garden grow?

(And Michael says)

With purple spoons and yellow stars
And green balls all in a row.

Language Arts: Listening

Listening to Each Other

Any unit on plants is likely to have a strong scientific focus. As children plant seeds, sprout lima beans, and grow plants, they ask many questions, some of which are not easy to answer, such as: Why does the sun shine? What do our plants do at night when we're gone? Why does too much water turn plants yellow? Many of the questions you will probably be able to answer, but that doesn't mean you should answer them right away; instead, when interesting questions pop up, encourage the whole class to think about them. Accept all answers, not just "correct" ones; encourage the children to listen carefully to each other's ideas. Praise the children's thoughtfulness and, when appropriate, guide them toward the correct answer. Sometimes, however, you might not need to conclude a discussion with a scientific answer; for kindergartners, imaginative answers may suffice.

DO LEAVES HURT WHEN THEY DROOP?

Recommended Read-Aloud Books

□ *Grandma's House,* Moore (Lothrop)—A little girl spends the summer at her grandmother's house in the country.

□ *The Carrot Seed,* Krauss (Harper)—A boy plants a carrot seed and eventually gets a carrot.

□ *Miss Rumphius,* Cooney (Viking)—A charming woman plants lupine flower seeds around the countryside.

□ *The Legend of Bluebonnet,* dePaola (Putnam)—A Comanche girl's sacrifice brings the bluebonnet flower to Texas.

□ *Alligator's Garden,* Muntean and Rubel (Dial)—This story about an alligator who grows a garden is part of a playbook that contains a card game puzzle children can put together as you read the book.

□ *The Rose in My Garden,* Lobel (Greenwillow)—an add-on poem about flowers that shade a bee in the garden.

□ *Your First Garden Book,* Brown (Little, Brown)—an informational picture book for children.

Language Arts: Writing

Tree Diary

"Adopt" a tree outside of your school. Keep a class diary for the tree in a pad of language experience paper, making entries once a week. Each week have the children dictate how the tree looks, what the weather is like for the tree, and what animals are observed in and around the tree. Sometimes you might want to ask children to volunteer to write the dictation. (It doesn't matter if they do it correctly—the point is for them to have the experience of writing down someone else's words.) Have different children illustrate the diary each week. Save the pad in a special place for the children to "read" in their free time.

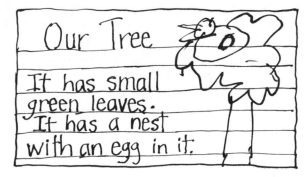

Flower and Fruit Names

Discuss again the names of the flowers in Mary's garden (see page 186): silver bells, cockleshells, and pretty maids. Talk about other interesting flower names—snapdragons, tiger lilies, buttercups, and bluebells—showing the children pictures of these flowers and asking them why they think the flowers are so named. Ask the children to list flower names that people have, such as Daisy, Flora, Marguerite, and Sweet Pea, and show them pictures for these flowers too. Ask them how they think the following fruits were named: orange, tangerine, plum, and peach. Make word cards of fruits and flowers for the children to copy in their writing. (See page 98 for information on making word cards.)

Language Arts: Reading

Sequence Stories

Take photographs of four-step processes in your class-room. For this unit, the processes are likely to involve plants growing. Make a bulletin board for the photographs, asking children to tell you the order in which to display them to show the proper sequence of the process. Make word cards to go under the pictures that say *first, next, then, finally.* Have the children draw their own picture sequences and label them *first, next, then,* and *finally.* Use these words frequently in class to discuss sequence. For a three-step sequence, drop one of the words after *first.* For a two-step process, drop two of the words after *first.* Encourage the children to "read" the pictures to tell stories about the processes they have used.

Social Studies

Classroom Farmers

CONCEPT: *A plant farmer's job is to plant new plants and take care of them.*

Set up a "farming" or "gardening" center on a table or counter near a window. Experiment with the children to find out what spot works best for growing plants and which plants grow best in your room. Provide in the center accessible planting equipment, such as jars, covers, water, toothpicks, potting soil, pebbles, paper cups, other containers, masking tape and pencils for labeling cups, and newspaper. Explaining that new plants can grow from old ones, demonstrate one planting project at a time, afterward letting children start that project on their own with avocado pits, sweet potatoes, or carrot tops they bring in from home. Teach them to clean up after themselves. If you like, "harvest" plants before vacation times, letting children take them home for good. Start new plants after vacation.

Carrot Plants. You need the tops of carrots (or beets) that have stems still on. Cut the stems back to one inch. Fill a shallow container with water. Sprinkle the bottom with small pebbles. Arrange carrot tops on top, stems up. Place in indirect light. Keep the pebbles and the bottom of the carrots wet. You should see new plant growth within a week.

Sweet Potato Plant. Place potato in container with toothpicks, as for avocado. Either end of the potato will do. After the roots have formed and the stem has appeared, plant in soil.

Avocado Plant. Dry the pit. Peel off the skin. Poke toothpicks into the pit, and set it over a cup of water, fat end down, so that the bottom is wet. Place in indirect light. Keep the bottom wet with frequent watering. In three weeks a root should grow down, and soon afterward a stem should grow up. Plant the pit in a pot, not quite burying the pit. When the stem is seven inches tall, cut it back halfway to make the plant branch.

Social Studies

Classroom Salad Chefs

CONCEPT: *A "chef" is someone who prepares food for others to eat.*

Explain that many people like to eat salads because they are healthful. Have the children pretend they are salad "chefs." Have them wash their hands, provide them with salad ingredients and paper plates, and help them make salads to eat in class. Let the children create their own recipes for salads, taking down their dictation for a class salad cookbook. Following is a salad that may interest them:

Science

Plant Seeds

Explain that seeds are baby plants. Have each child plant three to four zinnia seeds or marigold seeds in damp soil in paper cups. Follow the directions on the seed packages. In a week or two you should see some signs of growth. Have the children save their best one or two seedlings, pulling up the rest to prevent crowding, and perhaps donating seedlings carefully to other children whose seeds didn't sprout. If you want plants for Mother's Day gifts, start them ahead of time. Consult the seed packages to see how long the flowers will take to bloom.

Transplant Small Plants

If you haven't time to plant seeds for Mother's Day flowers, you can buy small plants at a garden center. Have each child transplant a small plant into a paper cup. Mark the cups with names on masking tape. Have the children grow the plants in class for a few weeks before taking them home. Question for discussion: What do plants need to live? (water, air, and food—usually found in the soil)

Sprout Lima Beans

Show each child how to curl a thin sponge or folded paper towel around the inside of a plastic cup. Help each child put two or three dried lima beans between the sponge and the cup, and then pour in enough water to dampen the sponge. Don't cover. Set in indirect sunlight, where the children can observe the beans each day to make sure the sponge is damp. Mark on the calendar when the limas begin to sprout. Elicit in discussion the observations that the beans send roots down and stems up. Question for discussion: How do the lima beans know which way is up? Good question. Let the children come up with their own imaginative answers. Take down their dictation and have them illustrate their "scientific" explanations.

Science

Celery Experiment

Serve celery sticks for a snack. While the children are eating the celery, encourage them to observe how the celery is made. Set a stalk of celery with leaves in a glass of red food coloring, slightly diluted. Have the children draw pictures of the celery as it is at this time. Write, or let them write, the word *before* on their pictures. Then ask the children to predict what will happen to the celery. Have them draw pictures of their predictions. Write, or let them write, the word *prediction* on their pictures. An hour or two later, have the children observe the changes in the celery. (The leaves should be brownish.) Cut crosswise across the stalk to observe cross-sections of the veins, which should be red. Elicit through discussion the concept that a celery stalk has veins (like tubes or straws) that carry liquids up to the leaves above. Record the results of the experiment with new pictures, labeled *after*. Have the children tape their pictures together in three-step sequences: before, prediction, after. Display and review the steps of the experiment.

Nature Activity Kits

Various nature activity kits are available from Insect Lore Products, Inc., P.O. Box 1535, Shafter, CA 93263. Write for a catalog or call (805) 746-6047. Among the materials available from Insect Lore Products are butterfly nets, ant farms, silkworms, frogs' eggs, praying mantises, bug cages, insect-catching plants, treecrabs, bird feeders, and a butterfly garden school kit. Similar science materials may also be available from other classroom suppliers such as Childcraft Education Corporation. (See appendix for address and phone number.)

The butterfly garden school kit contains a butterfly garden with a coupon to be returned for materials and larvae needed by each student to raise his or her own painted lady butterfly. You can also buy a less expensive kit for raising one class butterfly. Raising a real butterfly is a terrific, memorable experience that teaches children the meaning of sequencing and the life cycle.

Math

Counting Parts of Plants

Look at real flowers together. Record what the flowers look like with "scientific" drawings. Count the petals and leaves on flowers, and write the numbers on the drawings. If the flowers have too many petals to count, write *many* on the picture. Save the pictures, using them to practice classification. Ask the children: How many ways can you classify the flower pictures? Some ways are by number of petals, by number of leaves, by color, by shape, and by size.

Grow a Number

Have the class pick a lucky number. (Perhaps it should be five or six, the age of most of the children.) Wet a sponge and set it in a shallow dish. Sprinkle cress seeds in the shape of the lucky number on the sponge. Set the seeds in indirect sunlight. Have the children take turns checking the sponge each day to make sure it is damp but not too soggy. Teach them to water the dish, not the sponge, so that the sponge can soak up the water it needs. As the seeds sprout, they will lean toward the light. Ask the children why. (Seedlings like light; they need it; they seek it.) Turn the dish around every so often to keep the sprouts growing up straight. If any seeds grow out of place, weed them out.

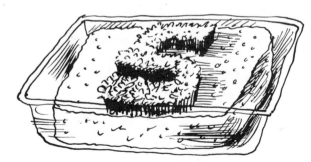

Math

Measure Real Plants

Have the children measure real plants as they grow with small blocks. Legos are good because they stack. Teach the children to stack the Legos next to the plants, count the Legos, and transfer the amount to a graph. Concept: *A graph is a picture of "how many."*

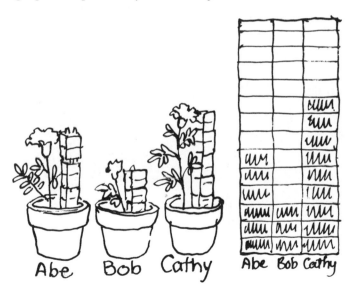

Measure a Magic Beanstalk

Plant a magic seed in class. Have the children think of what the seed should be (perhaps a small ball) and where they should plant it (perhaps in a basket of toys). Each day, ask a child to paint a new segment of the magic plant on a twelve-by-eighteen-inch piece of green construction paper. Hold the paper horizontally so the new segment is twelve inches (one foot high). This will make it easy to count how many feet long the beanstalk is each day. Tape the paintings together on the wall so that the beanstalk climbs up and around the room. Have the children write stories about their magic beanstalk. Be sure to read them "Jack and the Beanstalk."

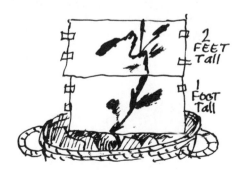

Art

How Many Ways Can We Make Flowers?

Provide the children with a variety of art materials, such as construction paper, small paper plates, glue, glitter, scissors, paint, markers, crayons, clay, yarn, telephone wire, twist ties, pipe cleaners, sticks, tissue paper, foil, and cellophane. You might also want to add junk materials, such as egg cartons (perhaps precut into one-cup sections), Styrofoam peanuts, cardboard tubes, and margarine containers. Ask the children to think of different ways to make flowers. Show them a few techniques, such as rolling a strip of paper around a pencil to curl it, making little wads of tissue paper and gluing them to egg carton cups, and sprinkling glitter on glue to make it sparkle. But in general, encourage creativity and a sharing of ideas. Attach flowers to pencils, florist stems, chopsticks, rulers, and dowels for stems. Make a class bouquet to decorate the room.

OUR
BOUQUET
OF
FLOWERS

Art

Photograms

To make photograms you need a special kind of light-sensitive paper called Solargraphics © paper, which you can order from school supply houses or Solargraphics, P.O. Box 7091P, Berkeley, CA 94707 (415-548-5230).

To make photograms, collect objects with interesting shapes from nature, such as leaves, grass, stems, and flowers. Place the objects on the Solargraphics paper, blue side up, on a tray or piece of cardboard for support. Place in direct sunlight for about three to seven minutes or until the blue paper turns white. In the shade, lay the paper in a pan of tap water for two minutes. The blue color will reappear, except where the objects made a silhouette. Dry on a flat surface. Flatten dried print by pressing between the pages of a big book overnight.

CLASSIFICATION PHOTOGRAMS: Ask the children to collect shapes that are not from nature, such as keys, lace, coins, paper clips, scissors, buttons, a pencil, and a comb. Help the children classify the objects they collect and plan photograms that contain objects that go together. Display the photograms so that other children can guess what the classifications are.

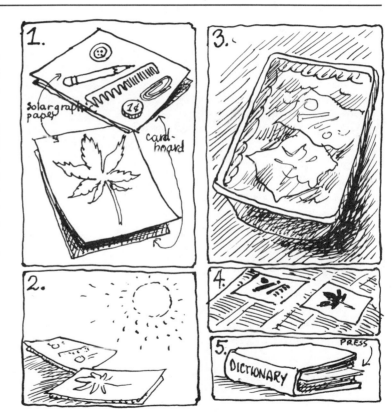

Music

Oats, Peas, Beans Circle Dance*

Chorus:

Oats, peas, beans, and barley grow,
Oats, peas, beans, and barley grow,
Do you, or I, or anyone know
How oats, peas, beans, and barley grow?

Verse:

First the farmer sows his seeds,
Then he stands and takes his ease.
Stamps his feet and claps his hands
And turns around to view the land.

If you like, substitute the child's name, as follows:

Farmer Betty sows her seeds,
Then she stands and takes her ease.
Stamps her feet and claps her hands
And turns around to view the land.

---

*Develop the meaning of the foods in the song by baking oatmeal cookies, serving barley soup with cooked peas and beans in it, and stuffing bean bags (you can use zip-lock plastic bags) with dried peas and beans.

Have the children join hands in a circle. Singing the chorus together, hold hands and walk around in a circle to the music. (If you don't know the tune, say it as a chant.) During the verse, everyone stands still and one child (farmer) goes to the center and acts out the verse.

Music

Flower Dance

Play Vivaldi's *Four Seasons,* and have the children create movements that represent various aspects of a flower's life: being seeds, sprouting, growing, waving in the breeze, being rained upon, forming buds, and flowering. Use scarves, crepe paper streamers, and flowers painted on paper plates for props. Encourage the children to contribute ideas for the fantasy ahead of time, writing their ideas on an experience chart as a story, which you can read them aloud during the musical creation.

Recommended Records and Tapes

☐ *Bean Bag Activities* (Kimbo).

☐ *One Light, One Sun* by Raffi.

Physical Education

A Tisket, A Tasket

A tisket, a tasket,
A green and yellow basket;
I wrote a letter to my love,
And on the way I lost it.
I lost it,
I lost it,
And on the way I lost it.
A little (boy, girl) picked it up
And put it in (his, her) pocket.*

Have the children join hands in a circle. One child (It) holds a handkerchief and walks around the outside of the circle, as the others sing. On the last "I lost it," It drops the handkerchief behind the nearest child and continues around the circle, this time walking quickly. Meanwhile, the child behind whom the handkerchief was dropped walks quickly in the opposite direction. The first one to get around the circle and pick up the handkerchief is the next It. Use your own discretion about allowing running.

*Help the children practice ahead of time saying the song and choosing the correct pronouns *his* and *her* for children in the class.

If you don't want the children to run, say that anyone who runs automatically loses the chance to be the next It.

NOTE: To connect this musical game with the theme of plants, do one of the following: (1) In a previous activity, have the children decorate paper with flowers to make stationery for writing letters to each other and then have someone deliver the letters to each other, carrying them around in a basket, or (2) substitute the third line "I wrote a letter to my love" with "I picked a flower for my love."

Physical Education

Inventing Bean Bag Games

Help the children make bean bags from zip-lock plastic bags or by sewing or stapling squares of cloth together and filling them with dried peas and beans. Explain that bean bags are an old-fashioned toy that probably their parents and grandparents played with when they were young. Discuss other kinds of things that could be put in bean bags: small pebbles, pinecones, sand, and Styrofoam peanuts. Ask What about water? to encourage critical thinking on the children's part.

Have the children help think up games to play with the bean bags they make. Explain that it's good for them to be able to invent games for themselves to play when they get bored. Write their ideas for games down on an experience chart and try them out. Encourage the children to change the rules of their games to improve them. Name the games according to the children who invented them, such as Mary's Bull's-eye Game and Johnny's Bean Bag Game.

Chapter 13

Theme: Animals

A good month in which to explore this theme is June because children can explore the topic outside. But animals are a good kindergarten topic all year round because children have a special interest in animals. A close look at the theme in June, then, should be the culmination of animal discussions that have taken place all year long, and many of the activities in this chapter can be done in earlier months (in a simpler or somewhat different way), then reviewed and repeated in June with more depth. The theme of animals connects well with the theme of growing up, an important topic for children as they get ready to leave kindergarten and enter first grade. Just as birds leave the nest, so do kindergartners become first-graders!

Today I brought your kittens to school for show 'n' tell.

Language Arts: Oral Language

Changing Words in Familiar Rhymes

Changing words in familiar fingerplays helps children listen to and reproduce sentence patterns.

Two little blackbirds sitting on a hill,
One named Jack.
One named Jill.
Fly away, Jack.
Fly away, Jill.
Come back, Jack.
Come back, Jill.

Ask the children to change the animals and their motions. For example, substitute *rabbits* and *hop* away.

Two little rabbits sitting on a hill,
One named Jack.
One named Jill.
Hop away, Jack.
Hop away, Jill.
Come back, Jack.
Come back, Jill.

For further variation, change the names *Jack* and *Jill* to other names. Help the children hear that the second name has to rhyme with *hill*. For example:

Two little horses standing on a hill,
One named Mary.
One named Will (or Bill or Phil).
Run away, Mary.
Run away, Will.
Come back, Mary.
Come back, Will.

 Two little magpies sitting on a hill...

 First comes Jack.

Then comes Jill.   Run away Jack.   Run away Jill.   Come back Jack.   Come back Jill!

Language Arts: Listening

Recordings of Animal Sounds

Make tape recordings of animal sounds. Ask the children to think of how many different kinds of animal sounds you could make together. Here are some ideas:

1. Record real animals making sounds at the zoo.

2. Have a Pets Day. Invite parents to come to school in the morning with their children and their pets (in cages, tanks, or on leashes). Make a tape recording of the sounds the pets make.

3. Record children saying the words we have for animal sounds, such as *bow-wow* for dogs. Ask, Do dogs really say *bow-wow*?

4. Record the children reciting the following poem (hold up pictures to signal each verse):

Bow-wow, says the dog;
Mew-mew, says the cat;
Grunt-grunt, goes the hog;
And *squeak*, says the rat.
Tu-who, says the owl;
Caw-caw, goes the crow;
Quack, quack, goes the duck;
And *moo*, says the cow.

Author Unknown

Recommended Read-Aloud Books

☐ *The Very Hungry Caterpillar,* Carle (Collins)—A caterpillar "eats" his way through the book and becomes . . .

☐ *Good Morning, Chick,* Ginsburg (Greenwillow)—A chick is taught how to take care of itself.

☐ *The Year at Maple Hill Farm,* Provenson (Atheneum)—a big book full of interesting pictures and descriptions.

☐ *Crow Boy,* Yashima (Viking)—A lonely boy reveals his talent for making wonderful crow sounds.

☐ *Who Lives Here?* Barlowe (Random House)—realistic illustrations of different animals in their homes.

☐ *Buggy Riddles* and *Fishy Riddles,* Hall and Eisenberg (Dial)—two easy-to-read books containing funny riddles about bugs and fish.

☐ *Once There Were No Pandas,* Greaves (Dutton)—the legend of how a girl's sacrifice brings about the appearance of pandas in China.

☐ *Jack Jump Under the Candelstick,* Pape (Albert Whitman)—story of a girl who sings nursery rhymes wrong on purpose.

☐ *Charlie Needs a Cloak,* de Paola (Prentice-Hall)—a good story that tells of the story of how a sheep's wool is made into clothing.

Language Arts: Writing

Five-Step Animal Poems

Have the children dictate poems for different animals you study. Explain that the poems do not have to rhyme, but that they do have to sound good and contain interesting words. Each poem has five lines, following a pattern.

Line 1: the name of the animal

Line 2: color and size of animal

Line 3: important body parts

Line 4: what the animal likes to eat

Line 5: the name of the animal (repeated)

For example:

Horse.
Brown and big.
Legs, mane, tail.
Grass, hay, oats.
Horse.

If you like, ask the children to dictate whole sentences for the lines, such as:

I see a cow.
The cow is black and white.
The cow has an udder.
The cow eats grass.
I see a cow.

Write the poems on an experience chart, illustrating each one with a picture to help the children remember it. Make copies of the poems for the children to illustrate, collate, and take home as class poetry books.

Language Arts: Reading

Animal Alphabet

Print the alphabet on the board or on a language experience chart, with the children saying the letters as you print them. Then ask them to name animals, one by one. Ask them to see if they can hear the first sound of each name and to tell you the letter that makes that sound. After they figure out the initial letter and sound, have them find that letter on your list. Write the animal's name next to the letter with a little picture or cutout to help the children "read" the name. Keep the animal alphabet project going over a period of days, slowly adding animal names to the list. Ask the children to think of more animal names for "homework." See if you can find an animal name for every letter in the alphabet.

Aa ape	Nn newt
Bb bear	Oo octopus
Cc cat	Pp penguin
Dd dog	Qq quail
Ee elephant	Rr rabbit
Ff fish	Ss seal
Gg giraffe	Tt tadpole
Hh horse	Uu unicorn
Ii iguana	Vv vulture
Jj jellyfish	Ww walrus
Kk kangaroo	Xx xanthocephalus (yellow-headed blackbird)
Ll lion	Yy yak
Mm monkey	Zz zebra

Social Studies

Habitats

Explain to the children that animals live in different places or "habitats." Some habitats are sky, water (ocean, tidal pools, ponds, lakes), and land (desert, fields, jungle, and forest). With the children cover a bulletin board with different colors of construction paper to represent different habitats. Colors you might use are light blue for the sky (perhaps adding cotton balls for clouds), green or brown (choose a color that best matches your area or use different greens and browns to help the children distinguish between desert, field, jungle, and forest areas), and dark blue for the water. Have the children draw or cut out pictures of animals and pin them to the board in their habitats. Discuss the various animals and habitats. A good discussion question is: Which animals can go in different habitats? (Geese, for example, can walk on land, swim, and fly.) For a lesson on conservation and animal preservation, add pictures of buildings and roads to the land and ask: How do buildings and roads affect animals' habitats?

Theme: Animals

Social Studies

Pets, Farm Animals, and Wildlife

The activity on page 208 involves classifying animals on the basis of habitat. Another way to classify animals is by their dependence on people. Explain that animals can be divided into three groups: pets, farm animals, and wildlife (animals that live in the wild). Ask the children to look at the habitats bulletin board they made (page 208). Ask them to build a house and a barn in front of it with blocks. Then ask them to take off the bulletin board pictures of pets and farm animals and to put these animals in the correct place in the new block structures. Discuss the care that pets and farm animals need.

Encourage the children to tell about pets and farm animals they have. To extend the activity, make a graph of pets children have. Children who don't have pets can name pets they'd like to have or imaginary pets. Keep a class wildlife diary of wildlife observed in the school area.

Invite to class people who work with pets (pet store owners, breeders), farm animals (farmers, ranchers), or wildlife (wildlife officers, park rangers). Have the children show the guests their habitats display, and help the children prepare (ahead of time) questions to ask the visitors.

Science

Eggs and Nests

CONCEPTS: *Eggs protect animals before they are ready to be born. Nests protect eggs.*

Give the children plastic or paper eggs, asking them to pretend they are real eggs. Show pictures of animals that hatch from eggs (birds, turtles, and some snakes) and of nests. Ask the children to imagine and name pretend animals in their eggs. Provide them with art materials for making nests (string, yarn, twine, sticks, grass, clay, cotton balls, and so forth); you may want the children to collect natural nest-making materials outside. Have the children make nests for their eggs. Use box lids or cardboard as bases for the nests. Afterward, display the nests and eggs with labels that tell what's inside. Have the children tell and write stories about their eggs and what happens when the animals inside hatch.

If possible, hatch an egg in class. A Chick-U-Bator is available from Childcraft Education Corporation. (See appendix.)

Encourage children to bring in real birds' nests that are abandoned by birds or that have fallen to the ground. In class, take apart a real bird's nest together to find out what it's made of and how it's made.

CONCEPT: *People eat eggs, but not the ones that are going to hatch into animals.*

Ask How many ways can we cook an egg? Let the children experiment with egg beaters. Cook eggs on a hot plate or electric frying pan in class. Warn the children to stay away from the heat and cord.

WHAT HAPPENS WHEN YOU BEAT EGG WHITES?

Science

Classroom Pets

Classroom animals give children the opportunity to observe animals on a day-to-day basis and to experience in a concrete way the needs of animals for shelter, food, and oxygen.

Tropical fish require little care once you have an aquarium established properly. Children can help with the feeding and cleaning of the tank. They can contribute fish to the tank from time to time to learn how fish interact. Ask a local pet store owner to help you set up the tank and to visit the class someday to tell about his/her job.

Parakeets are playful and can be tamed. With patience, some can be taught to talk, an interesting experience for kindergartners. Be prepared to clean the cage often. Again, local pet store owners can be helpful with advice.

Gerbils (also hamsters) are great classroom pets. They need little care—their cage needs to be cleaned only once every several weeks—and a day's feeding is a few tablespoons of gerbil food. If parents are willing to take the offspring, keep a male and female so that you can raise babies—a memorable experience for children. Consult local pet store owners for advice.

Anthills are fascinating to children and allow them to see how communal animals operate. A giant ant farm is available from Childcraft. (See appendix.)

Childcraft also sells Habitrail, a hamster/gerbil add-on environment; an aquarium set; Critter Condo, a collection of three dome-shaped homes for ants; a chrysalis that transforms into a butterfly; and a miniature tropical forest. Excellent materials for raising butterflies and silkworms in the classroom are also available from Insect Lore. (See appendix.)

Math

Animals, Math, and Mother Goose

Use these poems as springboards for discussing math and animals. Perhaps make copies of them for the children to illustrate. Encourage the children to memorize the poems.

Hickety, pickety, my black hen,
She lays eggs for gentlemen;
Gentlemen come every day
To see what my black hen doth lay,
Sometimes nine and sometimes ten,
Hickety, pickety, my black hen.

(Use an egg carton and plastic eggs to count out nine and then ten eggs. Use the carton also to introduce the concept of a dozen.)

One, two, three, four, five,
I caught a fish alive.
Six, seven, eight, nine, ten,
But I let it go again.
Why did you let it go?
Because it bit my finger so.
Which finger did it bite?
The little one upon the right.

As I was going to St. Ives,
I met a man with seven wives.
Each wife had seven sacks,
Each sack had seven cats,
Each cat had seven kits.
Kits, cats, sacks, and wives,
How many were going to St. Ives?

(Act this poem out to find out the answer. Have one boy be the man going to St. Ives, another be the man he met, and seven girls be the wives. The answer is one. The other eight people and 2,744 cats are going the other way.)

Math

How Big?

Show the children pictures of wild animals and ask the children how big (or small) they think the animals are. Use lengths of yarn to estimate how long and tall each animal is. Label the estimates and tape the strings to the wall. Then find out how long and tall the animals really are by checking in a book about animals or an encyclopedia. Measure the real measurements with yarn and compare with the estimates. A good resource book for this project is *Animals, A Picture Book of Facts and Figures* by Tibor Gergely (McGraw-Hill).

Goldfish 3″ long

Prairie dog 14″ tall

Orangutan 4 1/2′ tall

Kodiak bear 10′ tall, standing

Giraffe 19′ tall

Blue whale 100′ long

How Many?

Ask the children to draw or cut out pictures of animals. Together, make a graph that shows how many legs animals have. The columns on the graph can be: 0, 1, 2, 3, 4, and MANY. Have the children paste their animal pictures on the graph under the right column. Help them discover that some animals have no legs, no animals have one leg, and that many animals have two, four, or many legs. No animals have three legs except for four-legged animals who have lost a leg.

Art

Four Animal Art Projects

1. Wrapping Paper. You can make this by printing on tissue paper with animal cookie cutters dipped in tempera paint.

2. Purple Cows. Paint these to illustrate the poem by Gelett Burgess:

I never saw a purple cow,
  I never hope to see one;
But I can tell you anyhow,
  I'd rather see than be one.

3. Finger-paint Fish. Paint scales on paper. When dry, cut out fish shapes from the paper. Add eyes with stickers or markers. Decorate a wall or window with the fish. Have the children cut out and add plant shapes at the bottom to give a sense of the ocean floor.

4. Fancy Animal Tails. These are for dramatic fantasies. Provide string, ribbon, yarn, crepe paper, and strips of fabric for the tails. Encourage the children to use their imaginations to make the tails realistic or fanciful. Show them techniques for braiding tails and gluing on feathers and/or glitter.

INVENT FANCY FISH TAILS

Art

Papier-Mâché Animals

Plan several days for this project. On day one have the children build animals from junk sculpture materials: plastic containers, boxes, tubes, egg cartons, Styrofoam peanuts, and so forth. Have them build the animals on box lids turned upside down for bases. The animals can be realistic or imaginary. On day two make papier-mâché as follows: Mix flour and water to the consistency of thick cream. Cut or rip newspapers into strips one inch by six inches. Work on tables covered with newspapers. Show the children how to dip a strip of cut paper into the flour/water mixture and then pull it between two fingers to remove most of the moisture. Lay the strip on the sculpture. Continue to do this until all of the sculpture is covered with several layers of papier-mâché. Dry thoroughly and paint with poster paint. Label the bases with the animals' names, and tell or write stories about them.

215

Music

The Bear Went over the Mountain

The bear went over the mountain,
The bear went over the mountain,
The bear went over the mountain,
To see what he could see.

The other side of the mountain,
The other side of the mountain,
The other side of the mountain,
Was all that he could see.

Dramatize the song to music. Split the children into two groups and have them stand at opposite sides of an open space. Have one group of children sing "The Bear Went over the Mountain" as they pretend to march over a mountain in a line. When they finish singing both verses, they freeze. At this point, you suggest a new verse, such as, "The bear saw robins." At this point the other group of children imitate robins for the marchers to observe. The "robins" sing:

The bear saw robins,
The bear saw robins,
The bear saw robins,
Robins he could see.

At the end of their verse, the marchers and robins return to the opposite sides of the room, and you start over again, switching sides. The robins become the marchers, and the marchers become the next group of animals you name.

Music

Imitate Animal Movements

There are many ways to classify animals (see pages 208 and 209). Ask the children to think of the different ways: by habitat, by their relationship to people (pets, farm animals, wildlife), by size, by color, and by movement. The children are likely to think of more ways—good! Encourage them to continue to think of ways, and use some of the methods they suggest to classify classroom animal pictures and models.

Movement activities can be used to supplement or even introduce the question: How many different ways do animals move? Secretly, show pairs of children animal toys or pictures and ask them to imitate these animals to music for the rest of the children. Ask the watchers to guess the animals.

Recommended Records and Tapes

☐ *Walk Like the Animals* (Kimbo).

☐ *Baby Beluga* by Raffi.

☐ *Share It* by Rosenshontz.

☐ *Sea Gulls—Music for Rest and Relaxation* by Hap Palmer.

☐ *Birds, Beasts, Bugs, and Little Fishes* by Pete Seeger.

Make your own class tape of animal songs, such as "Old MacDonald Had a Farm," "I'm Bringing Home a Baby Bumblebee," "Eentsy Weentsy Spider," "Shoo Fly," "Mary Had a Little Lamb," "Over in the Meadow," "Pop Goes the Weasel," "I Know an Old Lady Who Swallowed a Fly," "Five Little Ducks," and "Bingo." If possible, make a songbook with the words to these songs for the children to take home and sing with parents. Have the children illustrate the songbook.

217

Physical Education

Run, Rabbits, Run!

Pick one or two children to be "foxes" or other predators. They go and sit in a "foxhole" at the far end of the playing area, with their backs toward everyone. The rest of the children are "rabbits" or other prey. The rabbits line up at the opposite end of the playing area, facing the backs of the foxes. When you yell, "Rabbits, go eat," the rabbits creep across the playing area toward the foxes. When you yell, "Run, rabbits, run!" the foxes jump up and chase the rabbits back to their starting line. Any rabbits who are caught by foxes become foxes. The last rabbit left can take your place, giving the commands "Rabbits, go eat" and "Run, rabbits, run!"

CONCEPTS TO DISCUSS: *Some animals eat other animals. These animals are called* predators. *The animals who are eaten are called* prey. *Some animals eat animals and plants, and others eat only plants. What animals eat is yet another way to classify animals.*

Pin the Pocket on the Kangaroo

Discuss the body parts of different animals in class, using pictures and models of animals. Compare animal body parts with human body parts, reviewing the names of people's body parts. Have the children think of different ways to play Pin the Tail on the Donkey. For example, they might want to play Pin the Pocket on the Kangaroo, Pin the Trunk on the Elephant, or Pin the Tusk on the Walrus. Have them paint animal pictures to use in the games.

CONCEPT TO DISCUSS: *Animals have different body parts.*

Physical Education

Bull's-Eye Toss

Use a real bull's-eye target or make one with concentric circles. Assign points to the circles. Have the children take turns throwing little balls of Fun-tak at it. The Fun-tak will stick to the target so you can see where it lands and how many points are earned. Don't bother to keep score; that makes the game too competitive for kindergartners. Just let them throw, say how many points they earned that time, and move on to the next player. Remove the Fun-tak ball each time. Have the children stand near enough to the target that they earn points most of the time.

CONCEPT TO DISCUSS: *A bull's-eye is a design that looks like the round part of an eye. It is made up of circles. The inside circle is the hardest one to hit and so is worth the most points.*

Fish for Presents

This is a good game to play at holiday time or at the end of the year, when you might want to give each child a present for going on to first grade. The present might be a pencil, pad, crayons, or small book. To make the "fishing pole," tie a string to a yardstick. At the other end of the string, attach a hook bent from a paper clip. Wrap the presents in tissue paper and ribbon, leaving "catchable" bows on the ribbons. To play, each child "fishes" for his/her present.

Appendix

Skills Taught in Kindergarten

The problem with listing skills is that the lists are too long to be easily usable and that they give the wrong impression. They imply that skills can be taught one at a time. But that's not how young children learn. A teacher may think she's teaching children to discriminate the color blue, but they may be learning something else: that the person next to them has a cold, that the teacher has a high voice, and that worksheets are boring. Children learn organically according to their own needs, not according to how skills are listed on a chart. Nevertheless, a list of skills is helpful for teachers in planning programs and for checking periodically to make sure children are learning skills in coordination with the curriculum. If you like, you can devise a report card to report on the acquisition of skills, but bear in mind that once a skills list is used as a form of assessment, teachers may "teach to the list" only and neglect other aspects of the whole child.

Please note that the following are not the only worthwhile skills to teach kindergartners. Other skills lists have more or fewer skills, some listed differently in different ways and in a different order.

Oral Language Skills

1. Listening
2. Speaking
3. Telling a story
4. Reciting rhymes
5. Expressing one's feelings and ideas

Perceptual Discrimination Skills

1. Recognizing and identifying shapes and colors
2. Finding hidden shapes in pictures

Auditory Discrimination Skills

1. Identifying rhyming words
2. Listening to instructions

Comparison Skills (also called Relational Concepts)

1. Understanding and using words that describe position (*over/under, on/under, up/down, in/out, between/next to/among,* etc.)
2. Understanding and using words that describe amount (*more/less/fewer/same, none/some/all, most/least,* etc.)
3. Understanding and using words that describe size (*big/little, short/tall/long, fat/thin,* etc.)
4. Understanding and using words that describe distance (*near/far, here/there*)
5. Understanding and using words that describe time (*before/after, first/last, fast/slow,* etc.)
6. Understanding and using comparatives (*big/bigger/biggest, near/nearer/nearest,* etc.)
7. Understanding and using opposites (*big/little, near/far, before/after,* etc.)
8. Understanding and using the concepts *same/different*

Classification Skills

1. Sorting according to size, form, function, and other categories
2. Classifying according to size, form, function, and other categories
3. Brainstorming (listing alternatives) different ways to classify things

Sequencing Skills

1. Putting things in order of amount (1 to 10 and 10 to 1)
2. Putting things in order of events in time (first/next/then/finally, first/second/third/fourth)

Letter Skills

1. Recognizing letters
2. Saying the alphabet
3. Auditory discrimination of pictures that begin with same sounds
4. Sound/letter association (phonics) for those children who are ready for it
5. Writing one's name
6. Writing one's ideas with pictures, scribbles, strings of unrelated letters, invented spelling, and/or correct spelling
7. Reading one's writing
8. Reading one's name
9. Reading certain sight words
10. Reading a rebus
11. Additional reading (for those who are ready)

Number Skills

1. Recognizing numbers
2. Writing numbers
3. Counting
4. Understanding what written and spoken numbers mean
5. Using numbers to sequence pictures
6. Using numbers to record amounts and measurements

7. Taking measurements with nonstandard units (same size blocks, yarn strips, etc.)
8. Identifying ways people use numbers
9. Simple addition and subtraction of concrete objects
10. Using numbers and counting to solve problems

Problem-solving Skills

1. Identifying problems (What's wrong here?)
2. Identifying solutions (How can we fix it?)
3. Evaluating and using solutions (What would be the best to do? How can we do it?)
4. Predicting outcomes (What will happen next?)
5. Inferring antecedent events (What happened?)
6. Telling cause and effect (First, that happened and that made this happen.)
7. Using the scientific method (predicting/hypothesizing, testing, observing, recording results)

Materials and Equipment

The following addresses and phone numbers are provided so that you can write or call for information and catalogs.

Educational Toys and Play Equipment

Childcraft Education Corporation
20 Kilmer Road
P.O. Box 3081
Edison, NJ 08818-3081
(800) 631-5652
In New Jersey (201) 572-6100

Community Playthings
Rifton, NY 12471

DLM Teaching Resources
P.O. Box 4000
One DLM Park
Allen, TX 75002
(800) 527-4747
In Texas (800) 442-4711

Chaselle School Supply &
New England School Supply
9645 Gerwig Lane
Columbia, MD 21046
(800) CHASELLE
In Maryland (800) 492-7840

Nature Activity Kits

Butterfly nets, silkworms, bug catchers, bug houses, and butterfly kits are available from:

Insect Lore Products, Inc.
P.O. Box 1535
Shafter, CA 93263
(805) 746-6047

Books, Magazines, and Records

Children's Book Publishers

Write publishers for their backlist catalogs, which list all of their books in print. Often there is a section in which books are organized by theme.

Big, Easel Books

Oversized storybooks, big enough for the entire class to see well, are available from Scholastic, Inc. You can obtain a catalog by writing to:
Big Books
Scholastic, Inc.
Box 7502
Jefferson City, MO 65102.

Magazines

The best children's magazine for kindergarten is *Let's Find Out*. I have to admit I'm biased; I've been editor of the magazine for fifteen years! For more information, write to me:

Jean Marzollo
Let's Find Out
Scholastic, Inc.
730 Broadway
New York, NY 10003

Children's Literature on Tape and Records

An excellent assortment of high-quality children's literature on cassette tape and records is available from:

Caedmon
1995 Broadway
New York, NY 10023
(800) 223-0420
In New York (212) 580-3400

Records and tapes also can be ordered from:

Childcraft Education Corporation
(See address above.)

Kimbo Educational
P.O. Box 477A
Long Branch, NJ 07740
(800) 631-2187
In New Jersey (201) 229-4949

Computer Software Programs for Kindergarten

The following computer software programs have been used successfully in kindergartens:

Muppet Learning Keys (Koala)
Puzzle Master (Springboard)
Newsroom (Broderbund)
Print Shop (Springboard)
Comparison Kitchen (DLM)
Number Farm (DLM)
Stickybear Numbers (Xerox)
Storymaker (Scholastic)

Index